CW01651739

LEARNING TO CARE
PERSON TO PERSON

LEARNING TO CARE
PERSON TO PERSON

P. S. BYRNE OBE MB CHB FRCGP
B. E. L. LONG MA

CHURCHILL LIVINGSTONE
EDINBURGH AND LONDON 1973

© LONGMAN GROUP LIMITED, 1973

All rights reserved. No part of this publication may be reproduced, stored in a retrieval system, or transmitted in any form or by any means, electronic, mechanical, photocopying, recording or otherwise, without the prior permission of the publishers (Churchill Livingstone, Teviot Place, Edinburgh)

ISBN 0 443 00999 6

610.7

Printed in Great Britain

PREFACE

This book is written for those who are obliged by their profession to add a teaching role to their other primary professional roles. For those who are in fact new part-time teachers or trainers working within the confines and discipline of a profession. It is written too for those whose professional life is concerned with delivering personal service to people, for the 'caring' professions, while specifically we have used the medical general practitioner as our model. It is not written for those who consider their primary task in life to be that of teaching. By the time an individual has become qualified as a teacher and has had some experience, all that is contained in this book should have become second nature.

In our context few trainers will be likely to have had the benefit of a one-year course of teacher or trainer training. They will also have already discovered that their main teaching situation is one in which a student is 'attached' to them for a short or long period, and that most of their teaching will be in the form of the one-to-one trainer/trainee relationship.

The basis of this book is hopefully well rooted in that variety of disciplines which contribute to the study of 'education'. In producing it the authors, both teachers at a University, are largely reviewing four years of study of the problems of the one-to-one learning situation, one of the most ancient and well worn of all but sadly one of the less well represented in educational literature.

It is the authors' belief that the theoretical content of training for a profession may well be best imparted in college-based courses. But when the objects of the attentions of that profession are people, the application of the content to real life learning situations is best first carried out in the one-to-one situation.

We freely admit that whilst much of the book accords with contemporary educational standpoints, some parts are quite divorced from them. We have reached our conclusions from our own experience of the use of the various teaching approaches after considering the feedback received from our friendly 'guinea pigs', and from the observations we have made. Even so we still rely to some extent on favourable 'gut feelings' about some of the situations in which we found ourselves. We have used these situations also for examples and for the development of suggestions.

We would like to thank Mr Ray Taylor for his help with the illustrations.

CONTENTS

Chapter 1

INTRODUCTION

'The principal goal of education is to create men capable of doing new things, not simply repeating what other generations have done.'

Jean Piaget.

Changing fast in a fast changing world, general practice is attempting, as are younger 'caring' professions, to produce people capable of doing new things. To do so requires firstly new definitions of general practice relevant to contemporary and future community needs. Until these definitions are made, accepted and set out in educational terms, rational educational programmes cannot commence. Secondly, there emerges the uncomfortable difficulty that not only must the undergraduate or traineee learn to do new things, but so also must his general practitioner teacher. For a major weakness of general practice lies in the deficit of teachers with adequate resources and training for this new additional considered vocation.

Consultants, especially in the teaching hospitals, have all a long experience of formal teaching to a variety of students, undergraduates and postgraduates in medicine and allied disciplines. Few indeed of these consultants have enjoyed any educational programmes calculated to improve their effectiveness as teachers. At the same time, the majority discharge the Hippocratic duty to teach and maintain their personal effectiveness as teachers, by constant practice in transmitting their knowledge of, and experience in the fields in which they have assured expertise.

Even so, there is a growing awareness in their ranks, and particularly in medical schools, that modern educational theory and practice have much to contribute to the facilitation of medical learning. In one sense, the potential general practitioner teacher has a great deal more leeway to make up, lacking as he does any experience in formal teaching. Some consolation may be derived, however, from the thought that at least he has little to unlearn in the way of natural or experientially conditioned errors of teaching methods or style. He is free to learn his new trade of teacher, assured of finding ready help, advice and teaching from educationists.

Educationally he represents virgin soil, to be cultivated and profitably cropped in practical training. He is further free to select from the choice provided those ideas of style and method which best suit his personality and requirements. He is, moreover, by virtue of his chosen wide experience of people, eminently capable of making a rational and effective selection once he has become aware of what is available.

From our association of educationists and general practitioner teachers in Manchester we have come to learn that the behavioural skills of the latter, while still ill-defined, together constitute much of what has been termed the art of medicine. It is the conscious and selective use of these skills which proves to be at least as important as factual knowledge and physical skills in determining effective performances as a general practitioner.

We have evidence (Byrne and Freeman, 1970) to show that as far as postgraduate trainees are concerned, the general practitioner trainer has little, if anything, new to offer them in terms of clinical factual recall, at least in the areas we have measured. Where the trainer scores heavily is in the areas of patient relationships, management, manipulation and problem solving, the very areas where his empirical behavioural skills are ably demonstrated even if not understood by the demonstrator himself.

At this point, much further work is needed before the complex range of behavioural skills may be displayed. What seems important to us is that, even in advance of such definitions, just as urgently required in other 'caring' professions, all these potential teachers should become aware of the possibilities for the teaching/learning of behavioural skills.

This book then has been written for those in the various 'caring' professions who are obliged, as part of their work, to train newcomers in some aspects of the discharge of that profession. The trainer will rarely have more than one trainee at a time, and perhaps the nearest equivalent in formal education is the personal tutorial system which obtains in some universities and colleges. For our purpose we will refer to the training relationship as an attachment, a kind of apprenticeship. This form of training is now regaining some general degree of popularity, but curiously, even though it is one of the oldest of all teaching situations, especially in medicine, there is little in the literature to assist the trainer to fulfil his roles.

Attachment, as we see it, is the placement of a trainee with a trainer who will normally continue the discharge of his profession, whilst at the same time paying considerable attention to the structuring of such experiences for the trainee as will enable that trainee to understand more fully the nature and practice of the profession which he is entering.

The 'trainer', therefore, is already an accepted member of a professional group, which considers him to be suitable to undertake some of the training of new members of that profession.

The 'trainee' is a person who has acquired the necessary qualifications for entry to the same profession, but who has to undergo experiential learning in order to become a full member of that profession.

In these definitions we have already offered a number of prejudgements. The attachment relationship is not, by any means, the only learning experience the trainee will undergo. As this book stems from experience in the profession of general practice within medicine, the trainee general practitioner may be cited as an example of what we are describing. He has already qualified as a doctor, in that he has graduated from a medical school and has become registered by the General Medical Council. He has opted to spend at least one further year attached to a selected and approved general practitioner trainer. The purpose of this form of attachment, therefore, should be not so much that the trainee shall learn of medicine but that he shall learn of the nature of general practice. In recent times competence in general practice has been in the main acquired by simply practising, thus learning by trial and error. In the attachment situation the trainee, hopefully, will acquire in a year or so what might otherwise have taken him much longer. He will be learning more about the application of medicine from his trainer and he will discover how a general practitioner away from medical school keeps abreast of medicine.

Similar considerations apply to the nature of such training in a number of other professions. For example, in the fields of social work, attachment to an experienced professional often follows a university degree in the social sciences. Some specialist training courses in professional social work like child care seek to mix the attachment with the basic theoretical content of the profession. Here the emphasis is not upon the learning of theory, but upon the nature of application.

Attachment has certain characteristics and important historical connotations. It appeared as a form of training in the early modern period in the traditional craft apprenticeship, but in medicine had ever been of value. Apprenticeship, or whatever term was used by various trades to describe their own form of training, started from the premise that the best way a young man might learn the secrets of a trade or craft was by his becoming an assistant to a master of that trade. By first-hand study he learned the master's techniques. Yet from the time of Hippocrates traditional medical education has leaned heavily upon apprenticeship. It is only in recent times with the greatly increasing number of graduates that the system is endangered, requiring support by other methods.

This system of training also served most of our economic needs for at least five centuries and only further began to break down when the industrial revolution caused a demand for certain types of skilled labour for which the supply did not exist. Apprenticeship took at least five years, and the new masters of cotton, coal and iron were not to wait so long.

So in the case of the cotton industry the best female operative often had delegated to her the function of having new recruits sit next to her so that they might learn the best possible forms of skills. This type of training has been termed 'sitting by Nellie'. Currently, in many places 'sitting by Nellie' is synonymous with 'bad training'. Nellie is a lady in some disrepute.

Yet this is unfair to Nellie. If one examines the potential of her training and investigates its strengths, it appears that 'sitting by Nellie' is in disrepute for wrong reasons. It has been claimed that she failed because even though she was the best operative she could not pass on her skills. It is also claimed that if she did pass on her expertise, she also passed on some of her in-built errors. It was further considered that the time she took to train another operative to her own level was prohibitively expensive.

There are fallacies in such judgements. How many readers have during their university or college careers suffered lectures by the 'leading authority in his field' only to discover that whilst he may well have been the leading authority, he was also a laggard in communication. The best teacher is often not the best exponent of a discipline. If an individual is being selected in order to train new members of a profession it should be appreciated that the ability to communicate is at least as important as expertise in the professional discipline. The highest level of task-expertise and the greatest ability to communicate are rarely to be found in the same person.

In the caring professions the definition of what constitutes the 'best doctor' or of what constitutes the 'best social worker' is largely a matter of opinion and viewpoint. The doctor's doctor may well not be the patient's doctor. In the caring professions, moreover, 'Nellie' is not merely demonstrating the physical skills of loom operation. People, clients, patients are so much more complex and it is commensurate behavioural patterns rather than physical skills which distinguish the 'mentor' doctor trainer from his trainees in the apprenticeship learning situation of general practice.

The master may pass on his mistakes to the apprentice but to do so is to some degree inevitable in any teaching situation. The alternative to apprenticeship or attachment is often the 'course' in which one trainer teaches several trainees. As any trainer is liable to error, all that has happened is that instead of mistakes being transmitted to one other, the course presents the opportunity to pass on mistakes to twenty. Yet courses have some distinct advantages. They are economically more viable, a lot of teaching can be seen to have taken place and the participants may be seen to have enjoyed themselves. Courses, however, also have drawbacks, not the least being that whilst a lot of teaching may have occurred, an equal amount of learning often has not. There is also confusion over what 'courses and teachers' can achieve. The expectation of 'teachers' and the expectation of 'learners' can easily be such that only the most marginal learning may take place. Some teachers have such limited teaching styles and methods at their disposal that most of their achievable objectives could be better reached in their absence by means of learning aids.

A barrier to the effectiveness of our teaching is created by a failure to decide whether a teacher is teaching 'about 'something, or whether he is attempting to teach someone to 'do' something. The distinction has long been clear in the teaching of technical subjects. No one would consider teaching a motor-mechanic how to strip a gearbox utilising only a classroom and a blackboard.

The division is not as clear in many other fields. The way in which we produce teachers raises a whole range of unanswered questions. Whilst we seem to spend a lot of time ensuring that teachers have considerable competence in the subject they propose to teach, we appear to spend little time developing their ability to teach that subject. We have not yet managed to distinguish the real difference between the content of a teaching session and the behavioural skills required to teach it. The same criticism may be laid at the doors of some teachers in medical disciplines. Many general practitioners claim that the crux of their work is the consultation. If that is true, how many teachers in general practice spend time with trainees analysing the content of their own consultations?

Some educationalists, especially those with an interest in vocational training, are now commencing to reappraise apprenticeship, which was, it is true, a slow process. It was considered, however, a sure one—a quality rather than a quantity process. In general practice the traditional value of attachment was reflected by the creation in 1951 of the Trainee Practitioner Scheme. Imaginative though it was, abuses by some individuals clouded the scheme with suspicions, which have not yet in some quarters been dispelled. The scheme suffered also from the twin mythology that all general practitioners are almost equal and that appointed trainers had all been effectively selected as good teachers. Indeed it has been said, perhaps unfairly, that in making appointments to medical schools the last capacities to be examined are the ability and motivation to teach.

Despite such strictures the scheme has demonstrated that there were and are superb general practitioner 'Nellies'. Sitting in or with or by them and working with them has enabled so many trainees to fulfil the purpose of attachment—the encapsulation of learning by training. We believe that many general practitioners may be helped to become better trainers by learning of training methods and then training. In the caring professions generally all the signs are that more and more training will take place in the future.

We may now ask, 'When a trainee is attached to a trainer, what is the trainer setting out to achieve?' The trainer and trainee are coming together in attachment not merely for the trainee to learn about medicine. A major difference between the two parties is that the trainer has behind him a number of years of experience in the discharge of his profession. Thus, we would repeat that one of the major aims of the attachment should be an attempt to encapsulate into a period of a year or so what might have taken many years to learn. We suggest that whilst the trainee has much knowledge, he has yet to learn how to apply that knowledge to his work situation. This is the major reason for the attachment.

Some learning objectives are equally apparent. One feature of all the caring professions is that they involve direct dealings with people. It is reasonable to suggest that the idea of dealing with everyone in the same way is outmoded. A current belief is that such a professional should adjust his behaviour to suit the needs of the individual with whom he is dealing and not, as in many bureaucracies, vice versa. In general little is known about the development of new behaviour patterns or the modification of existing patterns in the trainee, but it is known that under certain circumstances it is possible both to learn new behaviours and to modify existing ones.

We return to the problem of the trainer and how he sees himself. It seems that he cannot be, in the case of general practice, merely a teacher of factual medicine. In the case of social work training the trainer is not a teacher of social work theory. This may be difficult for some general practitioner teachers to accept, especially as they themselves have never received training in behavioural patterns. One cannot conceive a general practice without medicine but it is with a small differential in clinical factual recall that effective attachment starts.

This does not mean that the content of conventional clinical medicine can be ignored in training. Far from it. If, for example, the trainee does not know the signs and symptoms of scarlet fever, and he is faced with such a case, then somehow they must be taught before he may deal effectively with a sufferer from this condition. The issue of 'medical content' will often occur, but the approach to the actual 'teaching' of this content may be handled in a variety of ways other than by simply 'telling'.

Most attachment situations will be those involving one trainer and one trainee. The trainees will have certain characteristics which influence the trainer/trainee relationship. In the first place they are mature, in that they are already some years into adulthood. This maturity factor suggests that they should not be subjected to learning situations which are primarily appropriate to children or adolescents. There will be problems, because most of the first generation of trainers in this situation will act upon their own ideas and their recollections of their own teachers who used methods suitable for children and adolescents often in medical school. All the same, teachers or trainers of adults may learn from the primary school classroom. As will be noted later, we advocate the frequent use of the 'discovery method'. 'Discovery method' was originally devised for use in primary schools. It happens that its application to the teaching of adults appears to be effective (O.E.C.D., 1969). It should be realised that the method as applied to primary school children looks quite different from the way in which it is applied to adults, especially when one considers the teacher/learner relationship.

The relationship between the two parties involved in the sort of learning situation we are discussing will suffer if the trainer fails to remember that he is more a teacher of application than of theory. In the case of general practice, for example, the trainee will quickly become aware should his grasp of factual medicine be better than that of his trainer. Teachers in schools and colleges may derive a great deal of security from the fact that they can always rely upon a considerable knowledge differential. The trainer in an attachment is likely to go sadly awry if he does not appreciate that his own differential is related more to his experience of application, rather than to his knowledge of the discipline.

No book may ever teach anybody how to teach. Effective teaching (and here we include training within the meaning of the word teaching) is largely a matter of knowledge of method and of content demonstrated through external expressions of the teacher's personality. It must depend as much on the personal enthusiasm and methodological competence of the teacher as it will on various qualities of the learner. All we may therefore offer to the reader are some ideas of the experientially gained beliefs about the teaching/learning situation, which a number of teachers and trainers of adults have found to be worth bearing in mind when they themselves approach such a situation.

In order to learn how to teach or train effectively, the professional would-be teacher has to gain experience and accept some sort of criticism of his performances. From such criticisms he may learn how to modify his own behaviour patterns in order to achieve greater effectiveness. In most activities, it is more learningful 'to do' than to be told 'about'. The telling about helps one not to make those mistakes which others have made, but effective personal techniques come only from practice. Thus we are concerned as much with 'task' as with 'process', i.e. the educational objectives and hence the content of learning derived from the discipline of general practice.

The 'process', the methods and styles of teaching adapted to learning situations, can be common to all disciplines where person to person teaching takes place. Each individual teacher in each of the several caring professions must define for himself the 'task'. We may indicate the possible forms of 'process' but in any learning situation the final choice is that of the teacher when he has become familiar with and practised in all. Even so, in the last analysis, the best teachers have competence, enthusiasm and flair; their own mastery of 'task' is more important than their use of 'process'. It is better for such rare gifted individuals that they read no further.

Chapter 2

THE LANGUAGE OF TRAINING

Most professional activities have their own specialised language which permits members of the profession to communicate in a specific sort of shorthand, thus speeding communication without losing anything because of incomprehension. Unfortunately the special language of 'training' has not developed to the point that it has an accepted universal meaning, yet it is worth learning for better communication and in order not to be deceived by those who have learned the words but not their meanings.

A useful starting point for this section is the use of the words 'teaching' and 'learning'. It is neither fashionable nor accurate to talk about teaching and teaching situations. It is more accurate to talk about learning facilitation and learning situations. There is also a flight from the use of the word 'teacher', exemplified in the statement 'I am not a teacher, I am a learning facilitator'.

The essential purpose of the profession of teaching is to facilitate learning so that it must be stressed that teaching and learning cannot be seen as separate activities. Teachers and students come together to indulge in a teaching/learning process. Normally teachers will teach and students will learn. Teachers can, however, teach and students can learn nothing, whilst it is also true that students may learn without any teaching going on (or, even worse, despite teaching).

The verb 'to teach' presents problems of interpretation if only because dictionary definitions are anything up to thirty years out of date. A common interpretation implies a positive activity in which somebody actively imparts something to somebody else. A more acceptable current interpretation of the verb would be 'causing somebody to learn'. One can cause people to learn by indirect as well as by one's own direct activity. A teacher can cause learning without actually imparting any of the desired learning himself. He may cause learning simply by telling the student to read a certain book. The teacher does not read the book, and then relate all its content to the student, neither does he read the book out loud to the student. None the less it is evident that the student can learn something as a result of his reading the book. The teacher has thus indirectly caused learning.

The teacher has wide control over the student's reading situation. He may recommend a specific article with title, page, volume and date, suggesting that he has specific learning goals in mind for his student. Alternatively, the student may be told to go into the library and find books on some more general problem. In the latter event the teacher only has control over the wide field within which the student is to select. Within that field the student may wander as he wishes.

Two of the terms used to define the methods of control, 'directive' and 'non-directive', are normally used in such a way that they represent poles of a spectrum of activity, ranging from the point at which the teacher is in total control of everything learned by the learner, to the point at which he is in only the most marginal control of what the learner may learn.

There is disagreement between educationists on the terms 'directive' and 'non-directive', and brisk exchanges may take place between those who claim to be 'non-directive' and those who claim to be 'directive'.

In an attempt to clarify the confusion it is worth indicating some of the problems of definition. In the first place all teachers and trainers should enter a learning situation with a learning objective in mind. Yet the range of objectives is vast. It runs from as simple an objective as that 'the student shall be able to recite the salient points of a particular piece of information, such as Hutchinson's triad of signs in congenital syphilis' to as complex an objective as 'to enable the student to identify the effects which his personality produces in another person during a face-to-face interaction'.

Teachers are directive when intervening to present new facts and concepts, or new interpretations of old facts and concepts. There are also occasions when teachers present matter which they believe to have been already learned, or partly learned, in order to 'reinforce' such existing learning.

Having decided which new matter to present and when to present it, they are also aware that this input has to have some effect upon the learner and they seek to control the effect as well.

While different teachers may have the same learning objectives for a given learning situation it is the way in which the teacher seeks to encourage the learner to achieve his learning that involves direction. An obvious way to teach somebody that two plus two equals four is simply to tell him that two plus two equals four. The same end may be achieved by presenting the learner with a number of objects, e.g. apples, and allowing him to discover for himself that two apples plus two apples equals four apples. In each case the result is the same—the learner has learned that two plus two equals four. It is the route by which the teacher contrives to make learning take place which is critically different. To a great extent the nature of 'directive' refers to the latitude in routing allowed to the learner in his pursuit of his required content of the learning situation. Thus 'directive' permits the less, 'non-directive' the more latitude, to the learner.

Now we come to the terms 'structured' and 'unstructured'. One may hear them used as synonyms for 'directive' and 'non-directive'. They cannot be so, because no teacher/learner situation is without some form of structure. Learning by doing so oneself without any external critique of how well one is performing is perhaps the only form of unstructured learning experience. The term 'structured' in a learning situation refers to the relationship between the learner, the teacher and the content to be learned. In teaching two plus two equals four the teacher may say to the learner, 'I am going to tell you that two plus two equals four. You have now learned that two plus two equals four. If you say to me that two plus two equals five or three you are wrong, because it equals four. I have now taught you that two plus two equals four.' In this situation the teacher has assumed control over the content, over the relationship of the student to the content, and over the relationship of the student to the teacher. The teacher is the central person in that particular teaching relationship. He is the arbiter of what is being learned, of how it is being learned, and of the relationship between himself and the learner. It is an authoritarian structure.

The teacher may alternatively give a number of apples to the learner and invite the learner to find out how many apples make four. The learning situation is quite differently structured. 'Two plus two' is a meaningless concept unless one can see to what 'two' actually refers. Thus the learning pattern has been restructured by the apples. Also the role relationship of the learner and the teacher has been restructured in that there is a greater degree of interplay possible between teacher and learner. While all learning situations then are structured, a very wide range of structures is open to teachers and learners.

Positive direction towards a specific learning objective has associated authoritarian structures. Freedom to select routes to a specific learning goals has associated non-authoritarian structures. It is wiser not to talk about unstructured learning situations but to consider a variety of structures in the context of 'directive' and 'non-directive' methodology.

We have previously referred to the concept of 'learning objectives'. Learning objectives are statements of what one is trying to help the learner to achieve in particular learning situations. They are normally expressed in behavioural terms. Thus, 'The learner shall be able to recite ten causes of hepatic enlargement.' The importance of expressing the objective in behavioural terms cannot be overemphasised. It is not enough to state that the 'learner ought to know', etc. If it is desired that he is able to produce ten causes of hepatic enlargement then the trainer will not know that the trainee does have this learning unless the trainee actually demonstrates it by reciting them.

The novice teacher will discover that the area of learning objectives has much more written material available than he is ever likely to need, or even to be able fully to understand. The most sophisticated and thorough work is the *Taxonomy of Educational Objectives* (Bloom, 1956), which is in three volumes and places all learning objectives into one of three categories or in Bloom's terms 'domains': the cognitive, affective and the psychomotor.

The 'cognitive' domain includes 'those objectives which deal with the recall or recognition of knowledge and the development of intellectual skills and abilities'. The 'affective domain' includes 'objectives which describe changes in interest, attitudes and values, and the development of appreciations and adequate adjustment'. The third and final 'domain' (not in print at the time of writing) is the 'psychomotor domain' which is concerned with manipulative and motor skills.

For those who wish to develop a wider understanding of educational objectives there is no work comparable with that of Bloom. For those who prefer not to accept his academic challenge however, simpler yet necessarily less precise versions exist, which despite their simplicity do help in formulating desired end products.

Professor John Morris of the Manchester Business School has offered a simple approach to examining educational objectives on a six-point scale. Morris postulates that one can site educational objectives within the following structures:

1. Physical skills
2. Knowledge
3. Use of knowledge and skills
4. Social skills
5. Interpersonal skills
6. Self-understanding.

This scale therefore runs from the highly concrete type of objective such as teaching somebody the physical skill of how to use a chisel or a simple piece of machinery, right through to highly abstract objectives such as to enable an individual to discover varying degrees of self-understanding. (Professor Morris is also co-author of three excellent volumes in this field. See Morris and Lunzer, 1968.)

Without embarking upon a long discussion of learning objectives it must be pointed out that no trainer should enter into a learning situation unless he is clear in his own mind what he wishes the trainee to achieve. If, for example, one is attempting to teach a general practitioner something of the interactions between himself and a patient in the consultation, or a caseworker something about the way in which they deal with a client, one must realise that in such a learning situation one is concerned with, *inter alia,* interpersonal skills.

The setting of objectives in the teaching/learning situation is a critical component of the trainer's task. Keuthe, in his book *The Teaching Learning Process* (Kuethe, 1968), considers this component from the learner's point of view. He points out that in learning situations which take place outside of schools learning itself is usually a by-product of an individual's efforts to reach certain goals, or of his taking part in some learning activity. 'Normally', writes Keuthe, 'the person's goal is not to learn, but to reach the stage of having acquired certain skills or goals. For example, regardless of what I may say I do not wish to learn Spanish; rather I want to be able to speak Spanish.'

Keuthe, who has written primarily for school teachers, displays a clear understanding of the adult learner. A child in school is prepared to accept those learning objectives laid down for him by the school system, and largely he is not in a position to question them. Until recently some university teachers have made the unwarranted assumption that their students are in a similar situation. If the school child knows, for example, what moved William to conquer England in 1066 he may have acquired knowledge which will help him to pass an examination. The adult student however demonstrates certain characteristics which distinguish him from school children. He has his own views on what sort of learning he wishes to achieve, and unless he has some sanction such as an examination conditioning him, he is unlikely to accept objectives which seem to him vague or irrelevant to his purpose. He is more concerned with learning how to do something or how to do something better. Thus if we wish to make our trainee a better general practitioner, it is important to discover what he considers a good general practitioner to be, and to what extent he sees himself to be deficient.

A further problem related to the setting of objectives in the attachment situation centres around what this situation can achieve, what the trainer wishes to achieve, and what the trainee may wish to achieve. We have stated our view that the attachment situation has little to do with the learning of theory and information dealt with by training schools and university departments. If we refer back to Morris's scale, our view is that the attachment has a great deal to do with social and interpersonal skills and with self-understanding. If the trainer discovers that the trainee is deficient in his knowledge then certainly he will have to respond to that deficiency, but it is neither his sole nor prime task to work at that level.

In the undergraduate curriculum students have had impressed upon them the importance of taking an adequate history. They are also taught why history-taking is important and are provided with routines of history-taking appropriate to particular types of case—the psychiatric and obstetric histories for example. The perceptive student may even discern for himself some of the behavioural skills required for successful history-taking, but in general such skills as the student obtains are acquired experientially. He is still ill-equipped with these skills when he himself is facing his own first unsupervised consultation. He is no longer dealing with 'cases' but with patients.

Part of our problem in training in behaviours is that, except in cases of a few isolated groups, such training has not been a recognised part of our national educational convention. Most of us have only had experience of learning knowledge and physical skills and we are conditioned to regard our teaching situations in the same light.

Curiously the theory on behaviour patterning has been available for a long time. One of the seminal texts in this field was produced in 1941 by Miller and Dollard. Despite its age, and even despite the fact that there have been so many developments in the field with which it is concerned, this book is continually being reprinted. Miller and Dollard discuss a type of learning which they describe as 'imitation'. Work in most professions concerned with people is characterised by some sort of social conformity and discipline derived from generations of experience and constituting a code of behaviour which the profession seeks to maintain. Newcomers to the profession lack insight into situations and do not recognise those cues which require certain responses.

To a degree there is a large component of imitation in attachment training. This is not to say that the trainer serves up a series of 'models' of behaviour which he expects the trainee totally to imitate. Imitation of this type may be true to many children but there is some doubt as to whether adults learn in the same way.

By the time a would-be general practitioner arrives for his period of postregistration attachment he will already have received a considerable degree of conditioning to much of his required professional behaviour. For years he will have been at risk to observe general practice as a patient himself and his modelling may well have started there. During his career through medical school he will have observed a long series of doctor/patient interactions conducted by his teachers. Yet his total life experience will have been in most medical schools as far as general practice is concerned, vicariously gained. His teachers at medical school are unlikely to have analysed for him their own behaviour with the patient, not least because they are more concerned with the pursuit of the objectives of the undergraduate curriculum.

Nonetheless the student will have acquired a number of pieces of learning which he considers valuable when creating his own behaviour models even for general practice. The period of attachment might be seen in part as a period in which the student, now a trainee, is encouraged to experiment with behaviour models in a variety of situations in which a desired result is an appreciation of his own role. The difference between 'training' and 'good old-fashioned experience' is that the trainee is in a position to receive some evaluation of his performance as soon as possible after its completion. This requirement further helps to explain the role of the trainer.

As we have used the term 'model' above, we should consider what it means in our context. When the trainer in attachment is working with patients, in the presence of his trainee, he is offering 'role models' to the trainee whether he, the trainer, appreciates it or not. Without the trainer being aware of it these offered models may be accepted or rejected by the trainee depending upon how they conform with his own views. Hence the trainee must be helped to realise that the study of such models is an essential part of his training. The trainee must also be made aware that the models are not being offered so that he may meekly adopt them, but that he may be able to observe each whole doctor/patient situation, consider how it was played out and then decide for himself what he will examine and/or adopt and what he will not.

The trainee's observation of models contains a number of problems for the trainer. As he is to some extent presenting himself for analysis the trainer may see attachment as containing personal risks for himself. Not infrequently able exponents of a skill are quite unable to explain how or why they do certain things within their skill activity. Equally the trainee may not be sufficiently aware of what he is observing to pick up all the essential cues which the experienced trainer discerns in a situation. As the relationship built up between the trainer and the trainee is critical, the trainer who sets himself up as an absolute authority in a complex discipline such as general practice, is not only lacking in essential humility, but is asking for more than a little trouble. The best trainers will recognise the value of their personal models to an individual trainee.

In some areas the lines drawn between types of learning are extremely difficult to discern. If we take as an example a doctor/patient situation in which the doctor is satisfied with the physical condition of the patient but is growing increasingly uneasy about the development of a social, family or occupational problem, the approaches he may use to open up the learning situation can be presented in a cognitive fashion. One approach might well be to ask the sort of question which obliges the patient to talk rather than simply to answer the question. This interaction may well be presented at one level as follows:

1. The trainee will learn to distinguish between closed-ended and open-ended questions.
2. By considering 'open-ended questions' the trainee will learn the use of 'reflected questioning'.
3. The trainee will learn the value of the doctor's silence as an effective device in certain consultation.

The formal teaching of this can be prepared in the form of selected reading, e.g. one might programme the reading as follows:
1. Benjamin. The question. In *The Helping Interview*, Ch. 5. Houghton Mifflin.
2. Rogers. *Client Centered Therapy*. Houghton Mifflin.
3. Benjamin. *The Helping Interview*, pp. 25–28. Houghton Mifflin.

At this point the trainee should, assuming he is motivated to read, have assimilated a lot of information and opinion on this particular area of learning.

In Bloom's terms we would have assisted his cognitive learning. The problem is that this learning is far from sufficient equipment to permit the trainee to acquit himself effectively in practice with real life patients. Somehow the trainer has to arrange a second learning programme which will translate the cognitive learning into effective behaviour. The trainee has to acquire the skill of using his knowledge. Thus we need to begin to be able to specify 'affective objectives'.

1. The trainee will learn to recognise and respond to verbal and non-verbal cues in patient behaviour which will indicate to him the possibility of the need for a deeper exploration of the patient's presenting problem.
2. The trainee will discover for himself the personal strains involved in remaining silent, when his instinct is to talk.

To use a crude but descriptive explanation of the differences in the process, the first set of objectives may be achieved by simply reading books and talking about the content of the book. The second set of objectives, however, are more adequately learned 'in the guts' than in the head. It is the feeling of experiences and learning from experiences which is so important here.

As we shall hope to show later, we believe in learning from experience, a great, if traditional, teacher. However, there are ways of simulating real life experience which achieve much experiential learning without an accompanying risk of the patient being harmed.

In the training process there are many opportunities within the confines of a normal surgery where insights may be achieved which reinforce the learning of behaviours. On more than one occasion during the teachers' courses at Manchester, doctors have commented upon how such learning objectives have been seen to be available in real life consultations. In these situations the trainer must realise that a trainee may well be identifying himself with his trainer who must continually ask himself the question, 'If I were in his position now what would I do?' On first 'hearing' an effective silence the trainee will be unlikely to have forgotten it, when subsequent to the patient leaving, his trainer asks him to comment upon 'silence'. The trainer will seek to help him in 'non-directive' ways to adapt models of behaviour to the trainee's own wishes and personality.

The term 'feedback' is widely used in the language of education. One essential aspect of 'feedback' is as a form of learning reinforcement, i.e. 'feedback' to the learner from the teacher. (*N.B.* the term 'reinforcement' has another meaning in educational psychology, which is not the meaning implied in this section.) It has been stated by many educational researchers that positive reinforcement following a response tends to increase the probability of that response occurring again. (For an excellent and simple introduction to the field of learning psychology see Evans, 1969.) In effect what is meant is that when a trainee does something which the trainer considers to have been done well, he simply informs the trainee that he approves. The act of offering approval produces in the trainee indications that what he did was, by his teacher's standards, acceptable. The giving of praise and reward is the main source of reinforcement.

Another important aspect of the area of feedback/reward is the development within the student of self-reward. Clearly, if a trainee performs a behaviour which draws from his trainer suitable rewards in the form of approval, the trainee's self-esteem is enhanced. It is then almost certain that his particular behaviour will be repeated, and that the trainee will think a lot better of himself.

In the field of behaviour development, however, we are faced with the problem that we are not simply concerned to get a trainee to model himself upon a trainer. Any trainer who believes that he is the perfect model for every trainee, in addition to being arrogant, might also question himself as to why he is teaching.

On so many occasions the behaviour pattern evolved by the student will be markedly different from that preferred by the trainer. Yet none of us, as teachers, are sufficiently perfect to be able to reward such deviations, on every occasion, with suitable feedback. The trainee must at some stage learn to reward himself through private reward systems which satisfy the needs of his own ego. Many adult learners can be seen to possess such systems, and in recognising this teachers must desist from destructive responses—if only because they may well damage the student's self-image.

This brings us to an examination of the concept of destructive feedback. If, for example, a student in the course of discussion produces a piece of information which is patently wrong, the bad teacher quickly makes certain that the student knows he is a fool.

Trainer: 'How would you provide information about contraception to a young Pakistani wife?'
Trainee: 'In the same way as I would advise a young English wife. The biological processes are just the same. I would give her the appropriate information.'

Here the trainer could say, 'You are a fool'. There are, however, other approaches.

Trainer: 'Are there any relevant cultural differences between England and Pakistan which may often affect the family?'
Trainee: 'Mmm . . . Yes. There the mother-in-law is often the dominant figure, I think. Of course, I would have to take her into consideration and seek her help. Otherwise my advice would not be taken.'
Trainer: 'Fair enough. That is broadly correct.'

The point of this interaction is that although the trainee has made an initial error he has subsequently been helped to reach the point desired by the trainer. The trainee's self-image is still intact. Most of us can look back upon similar experiences during our own educational trials and know just how we felt at the time. The bad trainer could have provided the trainee with destructive feedback by saying.

Trainer: 'Sure, the biological processes are the same, but mother-in-law isn't. You'd get nowhere fast if you merely told the wife. Mother-in-law would stop her taking your advice!'

The trainee feels now that he is a fool for attempting to solve the stated problem while ignoring information which he in fact already possessed. He demonstrated this when asked a question which made him reflect more deeply.

Feedback, in order to be fully effective, needs to be given as soon as possible after the completion of the desired activity. It is probably part of everyone's experience that at some time in their career through school or university they presented work only to have it returned fitfully marked some weeks later. The comments offered on the work could never be fully related to the original effort simply because the difference in time was too great.

For the teaching/learning experiences of attachment, feedback is the primary weapon in the trainer's arsenal. Learning about one's own behaviour requires feedback almost before the behaviour is completed. To a large extent the feedback will be verbal, although most trainers have mannerisms such as nods, winks, arm movements or body movements which trainees quickly learn to decipher. Thus in the construction of training experiences it is simply not sufficient to demonstrate a particular activity, and then say, 'Off you go lad and do it yourself'. Having observed the behaviour the trainee must then be allowed to experiment with it, and having experimented, taken part in some considerable discussion on his own behaviour. To some extent the learning of behaviour patterns has much in common with the learning of motor skills. It would hardly be considered good training to demonstrate how to strip a gear-box simply by doing it on a bench in front of students. The real learning comes when the student is allowed to try out such an activity for himself, and whilst so doing to be coached largely by the provision of feedback. So it is with the learning of behaviour patterns, only it is a much more complicated sort of learning.

Lack of feedback produces predictably undesirable effects. Numbered amongst these are the growth of anxiety, uncertainty and ultimately lack of motivation. Keuthe (*op. cit.*) asserts that the lack of feedback can easily be interpreted by the learner as a form of punishment, or even worse as destructive negative feedback. There are yet other aspects of 'feedback' of great importance. These include the effect of feedback in helping the teacher's own development, and the assistance which feedback from the learner affords the teacher in evaluating the effectiveness of his teaching. The aggregation of feedback from the several learners in a training programme is the major method by which the programmes themselves may be monitored and evaluated by the teachers. These aspects of feedback will be later discussed in the chapter on Evaluation.

Related to the concept of feedback are the concepts of 'progressive achievement' and 'progressive assessment'. Too often, trainees are presented with a learning task which appears to them to be so beyond their concepts of their own capacity that they lose heart. Complex and difficult tasks may usually be broken down into a series of simple tasks, and the trainee can be invited to fulfil each in turn. Much contemporary management training is based upon this concept. Trainees, heading for sophisticated ends are offered a series of experiences, in the early stages of which success is inevitable, and the feedback obviously encouraging. The will to go further is thus encouraged. The hurdles grow higher every time, but the ability of the hurdler to get over them, and more important, his belief in his own ability is increased with each success.

To a great extent feedback and its acceptance are very much related to the concept of 'trainer esteem'. Research has demonstrated that human beings tend to accept more readily information coming from prized or valued sources than they do from those which are not so highly valued. One experiment went so far as to allow a group of university students to hear a lecture from an unknown researcher, and then to hear a lecture on the same subject from a popular professor (Fulton, 1970). By prior arrangement the researcher gave straightforward fact and well reasoned opinion, whilst the professor offered a load of rubbish—which the students should have recognised as such. The students, however, rejected the researcher and believed the professor. The critical relationship between the trainer and the trainee by its very person to person nature, is much more personal than the relationship between a university lecturer and his class. Many of us have been preconditioned into accepting that respect and distance are necessary components of the teacher/student relationship. Some teachers who have tried to analyse this concept suggest that the teacher's need for distance might be related to his own insecurity. Unfortunately no research has really proven this hypothesis and it must remain questionable. Attachment teachers must accept the bitter pill that their own precious classroom models may be irrelevant to the task of training, while a stand taken upon the dignity of knowledge differential may lead to an undignified retreat.

It may be painful even to suggest that in the attachment situation both the trainer and the trainee must explore what their respective roles are going to be, because sadly the education world has here little to offer in the way of guidance. One way is to advise that Professor Jones' excellent essay in *Teaching on Equal Terms* should become essential reading (Rogers, 1969).

The final concept we wish to discuss in this section is that of 'meaningfulness'. Adults tend to be much more selective in what they are prepared to learn than are children, in that they apply tests of relevance to that which they are offered. In a sense here are two concepts bound up together. The first is that the attachment trainee will probably have some ideas of what he wants to learn, i.e. of that which is 'meaningful' to him. These ideas may or may not be correct, but the trainer should not act upon the assumption that his own view is correct and that the trainee's view is wrong. This is an almost perfect prescription for much teaching and little learning.

The second part of the concept is more important. Earlier we mentioned the possibility of breaking up complex learning goals into smaller component parts. Many activities when broken up in this way are incapable of assuming that degree of 'meaningfulness' to the learner which will motivate his learning activity. If activities have to be broken up, it is important that the learner is aware of why they are so broken up and what is the relationship of the individual part to the whole. Here again feedback is critical. All trainers must beware of meaningfulness.

Undoubtedly there is a range of opinion relating to most of the terms we have discussed in this chapter, and not all educationists will entirely agree with our views. From the point of view of the reader, however, we conceive it to be helpful to provide our definitions or indications of the meanings we will imply when the terms are used in following chapters.

CHAPTER 3

A MODEL FOR THE TRAINING PROCESS

In organising the material in this book we have tried to proceed logically through various discussions of essential theory into discussions of a range of methodology and finally into a discussion of approaches to evaluation. The purpose of this short section is to take an 'overview' of the total training process and attempt to organise it into a logical sequence of activities.

It is inevitable that the trainee must eventually have personal responsibility for his patient. Whilst this is true it does not mean that the trainer will simply hand over his case load to the trainee as soon as the training period begins, or for that matter at any other point in the process. One obvious purpose of attachment is that the learner shall come to grips with reality by being exposed to reality. If this were simple then there would be no point in writing this book. The problem with reality is that it is full of risk. There exist not only the risk that the learner may misinterpret the medical clues in a situation, and thus come to a wrong diagnosis and hence to wrong therapy, but also that he may mishandle the patient in such a way that harmful relationships may be produced, or physical harm be caused.

Models of the training process are almost as numerous as are writers about training; none, however, appear to present an adequate explanation of the attachment form of training. This type of training takes place at a point at which many consider themselves to be already fitted for the job in which they are being trained. It is usually a period consequent upon a professional (and often theoretical) training. Occasionally it may proceed alongside such training.

Our prime concern is with that form of training which follows a university training, but precedes full entry into a professional group.

We need a model which takes all these factors into account and seeks to organise 'experience' into some logical sequence.

In this diagram we have attempted to demonstrate the training process as a series of steps, each building upon the previous one. The sequence, based largely upon the pragmatic experience of several trainers, is not meant to be an infallible guide or a perfect prescription. Clearly each student and each trainer will operate in ways which suit

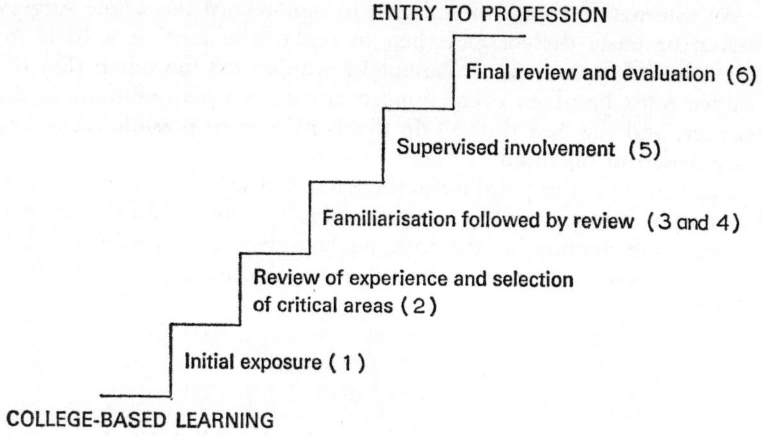

FIG. 1

them best. Each reader is thus invited to improve upon and amend the model as his own experience and personality sees fit.

Step 1 Initial exposure

In the first place we note that the entry into the cycle is postcollege, and that initially there is the simple exposure of the learner to the reality of the situation. He is at this stage a non-participant observer of the normal procedures of the profession he has opted to enter.

This, from the point of view of learning, is singularly important in that the learner will sometimes enter training with a possible range of misconceptions about what he is going into. He must, therefore, get as good a total view of the real situation as is possible.

This phase should not be overlengthy because the learner will have some enthusiasm which motivates him towards becoming himself involved in the actual situation. It would be highly demotivating if he were put into a corner of the consulting room for a fortnight and told to keep his mouth shut. Ideally he should expect to be a non-participant observer whilst the patient/client is consulting, but immediately after the patient/client has left the room, some opportunity for discussion should be found. One appreciates that in the case of general practitioners the pressures of any surgery may be such as to make this most difficult, but the general practitioner trainer has to realise that he not only has a responsibility to his patients who may be waiting, but that he also has a responsibility to his trainee. If one accepts the role of teacher, then one must also accept the responsibilities inherent in that role.

An alternative course of action is to tape-record the whole surgery session or parts thereof and then to replay the tape as a basis for discussion of its content. It cannot be emphasised too much that the trainee must be given every opportunity to put his questions to the teacher, and the best time to do this is as soon as possible after they have arisen in his mind.

The trainee at this point is not there to practise himself upon patients but simply to observe a teacher practising. It is important that he gets a clear introduction to the task he has elected to perform, while objective views are better formed from outside a situation than from within.

Step 2 Review of experience and selection of critical areas

(See section 'Deciding on learning programmes', chapter 5)

It is here that the teacher must clarify, both for himself and for the trainee, that the latter wishes to continue with his programme. It is also important that the trainer is prepared to handle those problems which may arise for the trainee should he happen to find that the reality of the situation is far removed from his preconceptions. At this point feelings are almost as important as logical presentations of fact. It might well be also that at this point the learner comes to the conclusion that he no longer wishes to pursue this particular aspect of his discipline and wants to opt for another branch. If that is the case then the teacher has to become a counsellor seeking to help the student to clarify his goals.

If this stage can be satisfactorily managed then from this point on the teacher is concerned with the real development of the student. Up to this point the teacher has had no need to be a formal teacher, but rather to be a demonstrator of normal professional skills.

Assuming then that the trainee wishes to continue it becomes appropriate to begin to discover what sort of learning programme may be constructed which will meet both the requirements of the teacher and of the trainee (see chapter 5 on agenda building). It will be said again and again in this book that the involvement of the learner in his own learning programme is of great importance. One is dealing with mature people who are already used to a degree of self-direction in their own lives. The purpose of the whole exercise is that they are enabled to become wholly self-directional and the best place to begin learning about self-direction is during training. Involvement in 'learning programme' design carries with it a responsibility for the fulfilment of the programme.

Step 3 Familiarisation

It is most difficult to write about this stage because it lends itself to the greatest degree of individual difference. We are suggesting here that trainers, knowing the areas in which they and their charges have decided to operate, can commence to examine various ways in which the learner can begin to explore without involving himself (or any patient) in real major risk. Most experienced trainers would agree that whilst a learner is in the process of learning some new behaviour pattern, a period of learning with relatively low risk is beneficial. This should never be taken to mean that the whole of the training process is without risk. Indeed the converse is nearer the truth. The purpose of attachment training can, in some ways, be explained as a device to reduce risks until the point at which the trainee is judged competent to stand on his own feet. In any profession where interactions between people represent the principal activity it is impossible that risk can be entirely eliminated. Thus risk must be included in the training process.

A useful technique which may be used in opening up step 3 is to present the learner with a role-play situation (q.v.) or, less risky, a simple open-ended case-study. This would need to be followed by a detailed discussion of what happened in the role play, so that the learner may receive as full a measure of feedback upon his performance as time allows. This stage may well even include participation with the trainer in the handling of a few carefully chosen patients.

No simple rules or guidelines can be offered in a book which will enable the trainer to know exactly how he should manage to get the trainee involved in a consultation. No doctor knows for certain what a patient is going to offer when he comes into the surgery, or when a doctor goes to the patient's bedside. The value of a good agenda-building session (step 2) can be seen here, because it will give the trainer a clear picture of what the trainee is looking for. Thus when something interesting or relevant presents itself the trainer has clear insights which will allow him to exploit the situation.

Step 4 Review of experience and agenda

This step is not so much a once-and-for-all activity which takes place when something has clearly come to an end. As will be noted in the chapter on agenda building, the nature of the whole training programme may well come under review at this stage. The trainer needs to be able to examine and re-examine the whole range of situations which have occurred. He must also regularly seek to encourage the trainee to review some of his own performances, and indeed his general direction (see Counselling, chapter 11).

At any time during the low-risk period the trainee may well have occasion to reassess his own ideas; while even more so the trainer will have occasion to reassess his own ideas. There is also a point to be made concerning a trainer's feelings about the trainee's initial agenda. The writers might well go so far as to allow their own trainees to build a programme known to be inadequate, and such an agenda could not be wholly satisfactory. But during the various reviews which may take place it is worth bearing in mind that subtle pressure may be brought to bear upon the trainee to get him to re-examine the programme on which he has decided. Various colleagues assure us that they have found 'counselling' to be a useful device in this context, as indeed we have found ourselves.

Steps 3, 4 and 5 are not necessarily offered as a simple sequential arrangement of learning experience. Some trainers prefer to view them as a set of interrelating activities which continue for a considerable length of time. In general practice attachment the potential for learning something new relates largely to the people seen in consultation. It seems probable that trainees will be oblivious to many possibilities before they start their training—and will wish to develop new learning as situations present it.

The trainer will wish to place the various areas of required learning according to some scale of relevance or complexity which he has devised with the trainee in mind. Consequently the initial agenda building is not a once-and-for-all activity but is related to the development of the overall content of a training programme. So a trainee may well have part-control of agreed activities whilst he is still building agendas in other areas of learning not yet covered. The trainer might wish, for example, to facilitate the trainee's further learning of clinical medicine before opening up the more difficult areas of interpersonal relationships, leaving the organisational and financial aspects of practice until later in the attachment.

Step 5 Supervised involvement

This step is a period of complete situation control by the trainee who works as the professional, but in the presence of his teacher. Unless he is clearly doing harm there should be no interruption of his management of each situation as it arises. Every situation, however, must be reviewed as soon as possible after the event. What is important however is that whilst the trainee knows that he is in full control of the situation, he knows also that his trainer is there to extract him from difficult situations should these arise (see Playing for real, chapter 12).

Step 6 Final review and evaluation

The trainee has now virtually reached a point at which he is going to be launched as a professional without the benefit of a trainer to correct his mistakes. Some of the content of this final review will be governed by whatever happened in previous reviews and appraisals. This review, however, is different because it may well be the last occasion when the trainer and his trainee will get together in the training relationship. It is essential that much of this review will be based on the trainee's perceptions of what he has learned, and thus it is essential that the trainer is fully conversant with the technique of non-directive counselling (q.v.). In the majority of professional settings the real judge of one's own performances is oneself. In the case of medicine and social work those criteria for the real appraisal of performance are so ill-defined that one is left with the view that one's own conscience is the important arbiter. The same is true of other fields. The fact that a teacher may enter upon a course of teacher training, and may perform brilliantly in a written examination tells us very little about his real ability to teach. The acid test of teacher training is not the written examination but performance in the classroom.

The final chapter in this book deals with modes of examination and appraisal. All of these techniques are valuable. The crucial question for a trainer to answer is, however, of a different order. What he really must know at the end is whether or not the trainee is capable of evaluating his own performance. Lastly, in discussing this step we suggest two important activities which ought to take place. The first ought to be a counselling-based examination by the trainee of his position. A second, which may not be necessary if the first is wholly successful, is an open and honest review by both parties of their feelings at that point in time. Not only does the trainer need to tell the trainee what he feels about the latter's performance, but also the trainee should be able to tell the teacher what he feels about his (the teacher's) performance. It is important for us as teachers to be prepared to receive such a review of our own performance so that we may continue to improve as teachers.

In summing up this chapter we repeat that the model must not be taken as an absolute prescription for the progress of all training situations. Situations will arise when trainers feel that trainees may well be allowed to jump quickly into real risk situations. Equally there will be other situations when the trainer conceives it to be necessary temporarily to remove his trainee from risk situations to limited risk or even simulated situations. These are the judgements which any teacher makes in the light of the situation in which he finds himself.

The ability to make these judgements is an important component of the professional skill and expertise of teachers.

To enable the trainer to make these judgements it is important to utilise time in order to discuss with the trainee his objectives and then continually to review them. It is easy to write about these steps in generalities but difficult to put them into practice. A frank, open and trusting relationship between both parties in which honest opinion may be given and taken is the vital component for success.

Chapter 4

TENETS FOR TEACHERS

In this short chapter we attempt to analyse the possible shifts of emphasis and control which may occur within well-known teaching situations.

It should now be clear that in discussing the relationship which exists between trainer and trainee, we are not talking about a single relationship, but about a whole range of relationships contained within the operation of trainer and trainee. From a theoretical standpoint we are also trying to offer ideas and models from a wide range of philosophic and psychological sources.

It is not uncommon to hear teachers involved in heated arguments over the degree to which one should allow learners to participate in teaching programmes. Sadly most of these debates rage at the level of personal feelings and do not proceed philosophically. In one approach, educational philosophy may be divided into three quite distinct camps, Socratic, Jesuitic and Heuristic—two old and traditional, one new and contemporary.

Broadly, Socratic teaching involves a highly informed, highly literate and philosophically inclined teacher encouraging students to find answers to problems from within their own reasoning processes. The teacher is a touchstone on which they test their ideas. In the last resort, however, the Socratic teacher is rarely wrong.

Jesuitic teaching is a model most of us easily recognise. It means a teacher who 'teaches'. Not only does he teach a mass of 'content', but he also has considerable influence over attitudes and values. Should one transgress then punishment follows as surely as it would have done if, as a child, one had decided to persist in the heresy that two plus two equals five.

Heuristic teaching is philosophically identified with Dewey (1961) and is certainly of the twentieth century, although its roots are older. Dewey places great emphasis upon the value of empirical approaches to all situations and experiential learning. He is not so much concerned to impose a value system upon his charges as to allow them, by their approach to life itself, to determine their own values (Dewey, 1959). For an introduction to Dewey see Frankena, 1965.

Clearly each reader will have a personal disposition towards one or other of these formulations. Our problem stems from the fact that each of these formulations has considerable implications for the actual behaviour of the teacher in each case. However, from another, more recent discipline—organisational psychology—we learn that behaviour patterns must often be modified to meet the behaviour of the learner. One might therefore conclude that to eliminate certain behaviours from our practice of teaching might preclude suitable interaction with students. One of the authors is, for example, much influenced by Dewey, but there are occasions upon which he opts to behave, even for a short time in an apparently Jesuitical manner. A similar proposition might be made about the general practitioner in his surgery. Even though he is completely identified with that group of practitioners who believe in the medicine of the whole person in a family, he would hardly start discussing family problems with a patient in the throes of a severe myocardial infarction. He must recognise that he has to adapt his strategy to the immediacy of the situation.

The field of educational psychology is even more bloodied by embattled argument over which approach is nearest to perfection. Sometimes one feels that educational psychologists are seeking perfect truth in a world made up of fantasies. For the pragmatic educationalist it is often safer to acknowledge all the formulations of the psychologists and then to find out if they work and, if so, in which situations they seem to work best.

Certain of the findings of psychologists are most useful to teachers and they may well be described as a series of tenets which are themselves based both upon research findings and the observations of practising teachers in practical situations.

For example we know that when a learner demonstrates that a behaviour desired by the teacher represents part or all of the objectives of a teaching/learning situation, then this manifestation of the learner must be met with a reward which will reinforce (Thompson and Hunnicutt, 1944). What we do not know is the exact nature of the form reinforcement reward should take. We do know that in certain cases teacher praise can be an effective reinforcer, but there also exists the possibility that an individual learner may well have his own inbuilt idiosyncratic self reward system.

Another relevant tenet for teachers concerns actually practising learned skills. If a learner has learned a new skill he will be better able to apply it to a variety of situations if he is allowed to spend some of his learning time practising the application of the new skill to the solving of problems. A most significant experiment in this area is that of Kersh in 1958. In his study Kersh established three groups of people each having to learn the same set of rules in order to solve mathematical problems. One group was a 'discovery group', another group was a totally 'taught' group, and the third group were enabled to learn by a method in between the other two. The results are fascinating, but for the totally 'teacher-centred' teacher ominous. The 'discovery' group were the most highly motivated group after the teaching, in that they displayed a considerable interest in the problems they were supposed to solve. The 'in-between' group, however, were the most successful at actually solving the problems.

This example provides a little insight into the outcomes of learning by discovery which also reinforces much other work done in the field. Discovery learners often do not learn the desired 'content' quite as well as groups which are given rather more support. However, 'discovery' taught individuals seem to retain for long periods a desire to go on discovering. The example further demonstrates the relative inefficiency of highly directive methods, even when the subject matter consists of straightforward mathematical rules (Shulman and Keislar, 1966).

An even more important tenet is the most problematic which asks one to accept as fact that all learners are different and have different learning capacities. Thus each individual learner should be learning within a programme which has been devised specifically for him. Equally, each learner will respond better, if at all, to some methods of teaching and will not respond well, if at all, to others. This tenet is not one which can be readily proven by reference to research. The writers, who are proponents of discovery learning, must admit that, under certain circumstances and with certain students, they have been forced to accept a student's demand for other methodological approaches. Some pioneering work in fitting courses to students is being undertaken at this moment by both the R.A.F. and the Army. The system being investigated is known as 'continuous flow' training, and has no set period for course completion. As yet, although initial results have been encouraging, no major research findings have been published.

Our finally offered tenet is perhaps that most fundamental to our approach. It is that a learner will learn behavioural responses much more effectively if he is encouraged to reason to make them for himself, rather than by reflecting his observations of some other person making specific responses. Those who doubt this are encouraged to read Skinner (1958). Clearly we are not suggesting that one should take a non-swimmer and throw him into the deep end of the pool on the basis that if he then swims he will have learned more effectively. Any learning activity, as we hope to show, can be prepared and led up to in a variety of ways, but one never knows how well one can swim unless the swimming is undertaken in competition or as an instance of *sauve qui peut.* In the training situation the final test of learning is when it is applied in the real life situation.

CHAPTER 5

TEACHING AND LEARNING IN ATTACHMENT

Deciding on learning programmes

We have already noted that one of the problems of teaching and training in an adult context, is the frequent disparity between what the student may wish to learn and what the teacher may wish to teach. Many teachers appear at times to be quite two-faced upon this issue. Although well aware that adults apply their own severe tests of relevance to learning situations, the teacher still often persists in pursuing his own unshared objectives. Also in the attachment situation there may well be a disparity between the purpose of the attachment and the actual objectives as pursued by the trainer. It is important for a general practitioner teacher to recognise at once that he is only partially engaged in teaching medicine in the sense that it is taught in a medical school. Equally a social worker with an attached student is not there to replicate what that student has already learned at college. The purpose of the attachment is to enable the trainee to examine the rules and application of medicine to general practice.

The academic learning content of general practice has been broadly defined by the Royal College of General Practitioners (1969) in 'The Educational Needs of the Future General Practitioner'.

In this short report the Council of this College states what it believes to be the content of training for general practice and the ways by which all future general practioners may be assured of obtaining this training.

A detailed development of this concise report will be published during the next year by the College. The present version states a concept of the general practitioner's role and demonstrates that he requires a special cluster of knowledge and skills; many of the individual items are shared with other doctors and other professions, but the whole is unique.

The general practitioner is a doctor who provides personal, primary and continuing medical care to individuals and families. He may attend his patients in their homes, in his consulting room, or sometimes in hospital. He accepts the responsibility for making an initial decision on every problem his patient may present to him, consulting with specialists when he thinks it appropriate to do so.

He will usually work in a group with other general practitioners, from premises that are built or modified for the purpose, with the help of para-medical colleagues, adequate secretarial staff and all the equipment which is necessary. Even if he is in single-handed practice, he will work in a team and delegate when necessary.

His diagnoses will be composed in physical, psychological and social terms. He will intervene therapeutically and educationally to promote his patients' health. (Task definition based on the work of Byrne and Freeman, 1969.)

The content of his educational needs falls into three areas—Clinical Medicine, physical, human development, human behaviour; Society and Medicine, and The Practice. Of these areas Clinical Medicine is the largest and most important.

AREA I CLINICAL MEDICINE

A. PHYSICAL

Appropriate expertise in traditional specialities, emphasising general medicine, and with special reference to:

a. The range of the 'normal'.
b. The patterns of illness.
c. The natural history of diseases.
d. Prevention.
e. Early diagnosis.
f. Diagnostic methods and techniques.
g. Management and treatment.

In the next three areas—human development, human behaviour, society and medicine—older doctors had little or no groundings as undergraduates. They do form part of undergraduate medical education today but their relevance to general practice warrants their further study.

B. HUMAN DEVELOPMENT

a. Genetics.
b. Foetal development.
c. Physical development in childhood, maturity and ageing.
d. Intellectual development in childhood, maturity and ageing.
e. Emotional development in childhood, maturity and ageing.
f. The range of the 'normal'.

C. HUMAN BEHAVIOUR

a. Social relationships—between individuals, within families, in school, at work, in other groups, and in the wider community.
b. The individual or family vulnerable because of medical or social situations, acute or chronic.
c. The meaning to the patient of his relationship and consultations with his general practitioner.
d. The general practitioner's role in accepting, understanding and advising on deviant behaviour patterns.

AREA II SOCIETY AND MEDICINE

a. The meanings of 'health' and 'illness'.
b. The relationship of medical services to other institutions of society.

c. The application of sociological and epidemiological principles to individuals and the practice community.
d. Interprofessional relationships in teamwork and consultation, delegation and referral.
e. The organisation of medical services in the United Kingdom, and comparison with those of other countries.

AREA III THE PRACTICE

a. Organisation
b. Premises, staffing and equipment.
c. Recording and communications.
d. Practice management.
e. Research methods.

These five areas also serve to indicate the needs of the individual for continuing education, and the opportunities for research either individual or co-operative.

This educational content, the 'task', is of itself largely sterile. It is the techniques of appropriate application, 'the process', which are equally important during the process of training. Both the trainer and the trainee are to be mutually concerned in task and process.

The wise trainer and trainee will together, at the commencement of attachment, seek to discover the latter's learning deficit, how far he is removed from full possession of the defined content.

Even when the trainer has his own objectives clear, there remains the basic problem of integrating the goals of the trainer with those of the trainee. In a face-to-face learning relationship any disparity of goal will seriously hinder the proper development of learning. Again we return to the point made by Kuethe about 'meaningfulness'. It is just not enough for the material involved to be understood by the trainer. The purpose of the learning activity is that the material is understood also by the trainee. This is a necessary statement of the obvious which must be stressed.

Important too is the self concept of the trainer. Most general practitioners have only limited experience of teaching roles, and sadly our experience of being taught has led us to the conclusion that many teachers desire to be gurus. Not surprisingly teachers who can be relied upon to be near infallible guides to knowledge and faultless sources of wisdom are so few. Infallibility is a highly fallible posture to adopt in attachment situations. Some who are able to conduct their teaching in front of large audiences can, if they desire, turn on party tricks or pose, like actors, for short periods of time. Few indeed even in this situation can maintain such a pose for long. The role-distance between the participants in formal teaching of large groups is in some ways a useful defence mechanism which does not exist in a person to person teaching situation. The audience is too close to the actor and can thus see through his paint.

We have also pointed out that in the attachment situation, especially the general practice attachment, it is possible that the trainee will know as much factually about the discipline of medicine as will his trainer. The trainee is, after all, much closer in time to his concentrated learning experience. We have also indicated that the trainee is not there simply to become a carbon copy of his trainer. He is in the attachment to develop himself into a member of a profession. The trainer is there to provide experiences, and resources which will allow the trainee to develop. He is not at any time a judge or a dictator preaching absolute values or fixed forms of behaviour.

Other parallels may be drawn with a variety of other professions. In industry, for example, it is not uncommon for a young graduate trainee to be attached for two years to a highly experienced and responsible senior manager. (Such a trainee may well be dignified with the title of P.A.) In this situation, especially if this is a technology based enterprise, the technological knowledge of the young graduate is likely to be greater and more up to date than that of his trainer. Technologies today (and in this context hospital medicine is in part a technology) are expanding at such a rate that it is estimated that the half life of a university training may well be only 10 years. Hence a general practitioner after 30 years of practice has only $12\frac{1}{2}$ per cent of his training to draw on, and is thus only as good as his reading of journals and texts, and the retention of material presented at courses and consultations.

What we are then suggesting is that the start of any attachment training programme be seen not as a plunge into the deep end, but as an exploratory examination of the pool which has to be covered. Each side in essence should declare itself and then mutually decide what it expects to achieve out of the situation. One of the prime purposes of this is to integrate the trainee into the management of his own learning situations. This may well be in sharp contrast to those experiences he has suffered in his own formal training. It also demonstrates to the trainee that he is no longer in the undergraduate category, but is an adult facing the responsibilities of adulthood.

The termination of attachment is often the point at which the trainee will go out into his profession and will there be expected to discharge his professional obligations as adequately as the most senior member of the profession. Thus one of the objectives of all professional training is bound up with the concept of responsibility. Responsibility is not something one assumes on the day one starts work, and the trainee may as well commence with that concept.

What can the trainer assume about his trainee which will help in the development of the attachment? An excellent analysis of the adult learner and his expectations is to be found in an essay by Professor H. A. Jones of Leicester (Rogers, 1969). Professor Jones isolates four characteristics of adults in the learning situation which one can agree are of critical importance.

1. *They expect to be taught.* Trainees, raised on a one-way teaching system, are conditioned by their experiences. It may well come as a shock to them to be invited to participate in the planning of their own programme. If, however, the trainer accepts total responsibility for the development of his 'package' he will never allow the trainee to demonstrate that he too is capable of responsibility.

2. *Students expect teachers to demonstrate professionalism in teaching.* There may be a degree of confusion because teachers are known to be members of the profession and are expected to have a mastery of their discipline. The term 'professionalism' relates here to the teaching task which they are undertaking. Professionalism, however, is not another word for a display of massive subject-area competence played to the gallery. The test of real skill is when the teacher gets the learner to do things which the learner once felt to be beyond his ability.

3. *Students expect to be made to work.* Professor Jones was writing about volunteer learners in non-vocational adult settings. The attachment student is in the same position in that he too will have some expectation that he has to work. Students also expect teachers to make demands upon them. This is a crunch in the attachment situation, that the trainer requires the trainee to work and not to be a passive observer of situations. Professor Jones also points out that non-vocational students dropped out of classes because no demands were made upon them. The attachment trainee may also be in the position where he can vote with his feet, while he can and probably will become demotivated if he finds that he is not expected to do anything. In this context Professor Jones's final words are critical, 'His expectation that he will be made to work can be harnessed at the outset, or it can be stifled into passivity.'

4. *Students expect to be treated with due dignity* however much they may expect to be called on to work, and however well they respond to the demand. In many ways we are returning to the theme of feedback which is given to students on their progress. Patronising students, humiliating students and neglecting students are all ways of destroying relationships. 'Holding a balance between encouragement and correction, so that criticism is accepted as constructive and progress felt to be there throughout, is one of the teachers' most delicate tasks.'

These four reasonable assumptions which may be made about trainees have clear implications for the ways in which we, as teachers, may be expected to act. The inescapable underlying premise is the involvement of the trainee and the sooner it starts the better.

In the opening phases of the attachment we thus stress that the programme building activity should be a joint activity. There is no golden rule for the way in which a learning agenda should be built, but both parties should set off on a joint programme clearly aware of what each other's objectives are. The method of some trainers is to tell the trainee that they have no objectives and then to invite him to open a discussion on areas which they might together cover. Others prefer to make a clear statement of their own objectives and then set the trainee the task of presenting his own. Whichever way one approaches the situation there will be problems. Some trainees may well be sufficiently clear and articulate to present their own objectives, whilst others, overwhelmed at being involved in the creation of their own programmes, are lost for words. In other situations where the trainer starts off with a *tabula rasa* he finds that the trainee has so few ideas that unless he steps in there will be nothing left at the end to work on. What is important is that the trainer makes clear to the trainee what he, the trainer, wishes to cover, and at the same time the trainer gets a clear idea of what it is the trainee wishes to cover.

An alternative approach is for the trainer to plan an initial period of training during which the trainee is expected to put together his own ideas for the next period.

This process of joint consultation on the planning of the learning period is not a once-and-for-all affair. In order to manage the situation properly it is necessary to hold a series of regular programme reviews. These reviews have two major purposes.

Firstly, they are used to check on what it is the trainee thinks he has learned and how this accords with the trainer's intentions. As attachment is normally for a long period of up to a year the trainer must, from time to time, check up on the way in which his programme is working. The review would thus be concerned to get the trainee to start talking about what he has experienced in the previous period and what he thinks he has learned from that experience. Later on we shall deal at length with the technique of counselling which is a prime tool of the trainer at this point. During such reviews the trainee should be encouraged to do most of the talking because it is the trainee's experience with which the trainer must be concerned.

Secondly, the review is concerned with the continuation and modification of the agenda. An example which may illustrate the value of this process concerns a student of vocational training studying at a university, who declared a special interest in a particularly complex pattern of activity evolved in the U.S.A. but not wholly exported to the U.K. He wished to discover if the theoretical basis of the activity in the U.S.A. was culturally consistent with the U.K. environment. He was given the task of reading such literature as was available. He then made the decision to examine the way in which some of these ideas had been implemented in the U.K. He arranged a series of visits to various organisations and at the end considered himself well briefed on the subject. Emotionally he was riding high on the strength of his investigations, but in questioning he appeared to be extraordinarily vague on the details of certain aspects of the activity. According to the agreed development programme his next task was to formulate a pilot attempt to introduce some of these activities to a small firm in the U.K.

A series of questions by the trainer confirmed his view that something was missing from the research the student had done and the problem then was how to handle the fact that the student would have to go back to the written material before actually attempting to implement any of his ideas. The trainer, however, also had to deal with the problem that the student felt himself to be fully aware of all the factors and was very satisfied with his own performance. Clearly the agenda had to be reappraised before any real-life risks could be envisaged.

In this case the solution was to get the student to prepare his plan of action, but with specific reference to some of the texts which were critical in the trainer's mind. The student was able to read this situation as a continuation of his project, whilst the trainer was able to feel some security in the fact that a re-reading of the material would bring the inconsistencies to light. The student was in fact able to 'discover' his errors without having to be told that errors existed.

This example has clear analogies in many situations. The trainee general practitioner will sooner rather than later conduct patient consultations by himself. He will have observed consultations conducted by his trainer and will have discussed them with him. One purpose of these discussions is to enable the trainer to be as certain as he can be that when the trainee conducts a consultation by himself:

1. He is going to make a reasonable job of it
2. He is not going to alienate the patient
3. He is not going to cause problems for the practice
4. He is not going to cause problems for his trainer.

The questions of patient management will loom large in training for general practice. The achievement by the trainee of successful patient management will be one of the primary purposes of training. It will be learned by observation, participation, review and by experimentation. Without reviews the only feedback to the trainee would be the patient's reactions which he would obtain only in a service as opposed to a training situation. The patient's reactions, while important and requiring interpretation, are not the only feedback on the conduct of patient management.

Another feature of reviews worth noting is that trainees may well discover within a few weeks a special clinical, or other interest. If that is the case (and it happens in nearly all extended learning programmes) the trainer should not insist upon the continuance of a programme which no longer meets the trainee's needs. Some mechanism is essential which will bring such a development out into the open to enable the trainer to modify his programme if he feels it is worth while.

We are not saying that a whole programme should be changed to accommodate a passing enthusiasm. We do suggest that if the trainee desires sufficiently strongly to pursue a special interest, then some accommodation must be made for that interest in his programme. There is nothing worse that a rigid fixed programme which becomes increasingly irrelevant to the needs of the trainee.

Reviews are necessary more frequently in the early stages of attachment or when changes in the programme are made due, for example, to the emergence of a new interest of the trainee.

For the trainer, the review is a valuable source of feedback on his teaching effectiveness. If an unaccustomed trainer, he must be prepared to learn of his teaching strengths and weaknesses as they affect his individual trainee. Even when accustomed to training he must avoid being smug or relying on familiar methods to work with an unusual trainee.

EXAMPLES

REVIEW

After eight weeks of 'sitting in' with his trainer, a trainee reacted to his frustration by having a row with him and walking out. It emerged that there had never been a real review of the situation. The trainee had not 'performed' in the sense that he himself had dealt with patients, hence his performance of the tasks (which he was in theory learning to perform) could not be assessed. The trainer had in his view regularly 'discussed' with the trainee the latter's 'performance'. The trainee considered rightly that he had only been 'told'—'watch what I do and one day you will be able to do it'. No young adult will ever learn how 'to do' in such a situation. The conflict might also have been avoided by an early real review and a genuine true initial discussion.

FLEXIBILITY OF PROGRAMMES

A trainee discovered a special interest in research after four months of attachment. It was an interest which the trainer did not share but he arranged with his trainee that the latter should attend a week's course on research in general practice. He also created opportunities for the trainee to visit practices in which research was taking place, liaising with the regional general practice adviser for this purpose. The trainee was able to enter practice as a principal with his interest sustained and with practical ideas for areas of future study.

In summary, in this chapter we have said that the attachment should preferably begin with a clear declaration by each party of what he seeks to achieve, and then, on this basis, a programme should be prepared which will plan the trainee's progress through an agreed phase of his attachment. At a given point in time this first phase should be reviewed by both parties in order to discover what has been learned by the trainee, so that his programme may be modified to meet any shortcomings or to include new developments.

Defining objectives

We have already referred to Morris's simplified and admittedly crude scale of educational objectives. It is also helpful when teachers wish to match their teaching methods and techniques to the objective, because it permits certain empirical judgements about the relationship between objective and method.

Most of the written work on this area is naturally concerned with classroom sized groups. We are concerned with groups which can fit into a surgery or a patient's bedroom—necessarily much smaller—and we are concerned in particular with the trainer/trainee situation of attachment.

There is little research into the working of such small groups compared with the vast amount relating to the working of larger groups. We have little more than pragmatic experience to guide us as to the teaching methods and techniques appropriate to the one-to-one teaching/learning situations. We can make statements such as 'classic lecture-type performances are inappropriate in the one-to-one setting', yet the validity of this statement rests upon our individual perception of the ludicrous in the concept of a lecturer upon a podium delivering to an audience of one, each embarrassed by the situation.

It is true that the dynamics of group discussions between eight or more people are quite different from those of discussions between two people. But most of us have spent more of our time discussing in groups of two, acquiring pragmatic skills in the setting. Discussion is a valuable teaching technique which ought to be developed.

In 1969, Long advocated a possible pattern of relationship between methods and objectives which followed the following lines (Long, 1969).

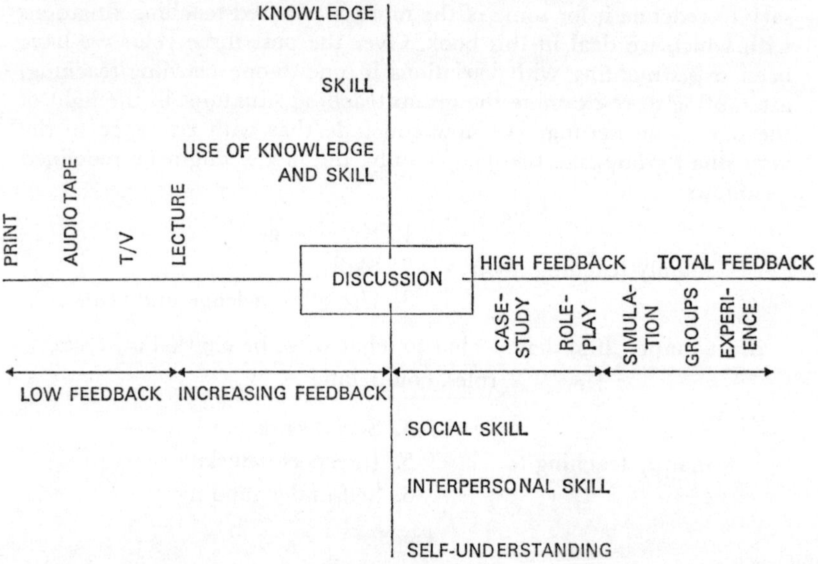

FIG. 2

The relationship advocated suggests that if one is dealing with knowledge or skill which the trainer has but the trainee does not share then initially one will have to rely upon more directive teaching techniques.

When one moves on to utilising either knowledge or skill or both, then it is necessary to use techniques which have a higher degree of feedback between teacher and learner, for example variations of the discussion method.

Below the line objectives, 'social skills, interpersonal skills and self-understanding', do not lend themselves to direct teaching in so far as they are matters for self-learning. The teacher therefore would seek to create situations within which this learning might take place. Therefore role playing, simulation and group learning seem to be appropriate in this type of objective.

Consequently one might argue that a crude relationship between method and objective exists along the line running from the top left-hand corner of the model to the bottom right-hand corner. Therefore if one is teaching interpersonal skills one would not be regarding lectures or print as the optimal media and equally if one were offering knowledge or skill one would not be using groups, because in both those situations negative correlations are suggested.

This model has been developed for use with groups and it is necessary to redefine it for some of the more specialised teaching situations with which we deal in this book. Over the past three years we have been experimenting with variations in one-to-one learning/teaching, attempting to re-examine the group teaching situations in the light of the one-to-one setting. We now conclude that with reference to the very small group, i.e. two people only, the model might be redefined as follows:

mainly teaching about {
1. Knowledge
2. Skills
3. Use of knowledge and skills

print tape film dem. chat to, chat with, be chatted at, cases, roles, counselling

mainly teaching to {
4. Social skills
5. Interpersonal skills
6. Self-understanding

FIG. 3

If we bear in mind a distinction we have already drawn between 'teaching about' and 'teaching to' we can begin to utilise these concepts in this setting.

As one progresses down the scale from knowledge to self-understanding the amount of teaching 'about' diminishes and the amount of teaching 'to' will increase. If a trainee demonstrates a clear lack of some knowledge or of a particular physical skill then these he must learn. There are a variety of ways in which he may learn, but in the main it is the teacher's task to ensure that the required content is both taught and learned.

In the context of most attachment learning situations the 'content' of any learning activity will usually be made up of items which are important to the discharge of the professional activity being learned. Thus all learning will be judged, both by the trainee and the trainer on the grounds of its utility. If some matter is considered to be useful then two sorts of learning are required. It is not enough to know the symptoms of diphtheria, i.e. learning 'about', one must also know how to use that knowledge—which we describe as 'learning to'—in making the diagnosis of diphtheria and then treating the disease. In Morris's scale (q.v.) learning is here taking place in the areas 1 and 3.

Before the progress to an analysis of the various types of learning area it is necessary to highlight the further use of this model for trainers. We would argue that learning areas 1 and (of Morris's scale) 2 are composed largely of matters which may be grouped under the heading of 'teaching and learning about'. Areas 3, 4, 5 and 6 are mainly composed of matters which may be grouped under the heading of 'teaching and learning to'. A better description might be that areas 1 and 2 contain learning objectives which the trainee may be 'taught' and thus learn. Areas 3, 4, 5 and 6 contain learning objectives which can only be 'learned' in learning situations contrived by the teacher and/or by experience. These statements are not always true of Morris's area 3, but may be taken, in relations to it, as a useful general guide.

In any learning situation the teacher is going to be presented with a spectrum of objectives which can fall into more than one of the indicated areas. For example, a large organisational component is contained in the running of a successful practice. Every successful practitioner will need to be something of a manager, something of an accountant and something of a personnel manager. He is in all senses the manager of a business. In order to run that business he will need detailed knowledge of, for example, record systems. He will also need to be able to use that knowledge in order to maintain his record system and to take advantage of it. He will also need to be able to train an ancillary in record keeping so that he may himself spend as little time as possible in routine paper work. We can draw up a learning programme for a trainee in this area utilising what we know about the relationship between methods and objectives.

In the first place we begin with the record card. Here the trainee needs knowledge.

1. What is a record card?
2. What is its function?
3. What sort of information does it carry?
4. How does this information help the practitioner?
5. What indexing system allows one to trace a particular card?
6. Who is responsible for the management of the particular indexing system?

All the above is in one sense 'knowledge'. As such it can be presented to the trainee in the form of a printed handout, or by telling him in the process of a 'chat'. As a variation the trainee might very well be presented with the record system and asked to 'discover' the answers to these questions for himself. This variation, however, could occupy too much time. The trainee may, of course, know already the answers to items 1, 2, 3 and 4. If this were found to be true then a strong argument could be advanced for allowing him to 'discover' the answers to the remaining questions.

Having discovered that the trainee knows the answers to these questions, the trainer must then find if the trainee is able to use his knowledge effectively. Thus:

1. Can he fill in a record card?
2. Does he fill it in in such a way that its contents are useful?
3. Can he use the information he has entered on a previous occasion?
4. Can he trace a record card?
5. Can he get somebody else to trace a record card?

Here is a situation where the trainee has to 'do' something. With the exception of the last question (5) the learning can be managed as part of his normal work when he can be required to perform all these functions in lieu of his trainer.

Item 5, however, leads us on to a quite different field. A practitioner should not normally expect to hunt around a filing system in order to find a card. Several times in his career, however, he will have had to explain to a new receptionist how this is to be done. Here we enter those fields where one is dealing with social or interpersonal skills. These are areas in which the trainer seeking to 'facilitate his trainee's learning' might well wish to look at the possibilities of simulating an experience by using a case study (q.v.) or a role-playing situation (q.v.). The management of ancillary workers is as sensitive an area of learning as is the management of patients. It is not possible to prescribe perfect rules and precepts for either. All one can do as a trainer is to 'create relevant situations' in which the learner may learn something of practice value.

This discussion of objectives is vitally important because we must make certain that what we are doing to the trainee is that which we intend to do. In any learning situation the teacher has objectives. Even a non-directive group leader has objectives. If one has no real objectives in a learning situation one is in the position of being on a train which is going somewhere, but one does no know where, and has come from somewhere but again one does not know whence.

Here is a simple system model to explain this concept:

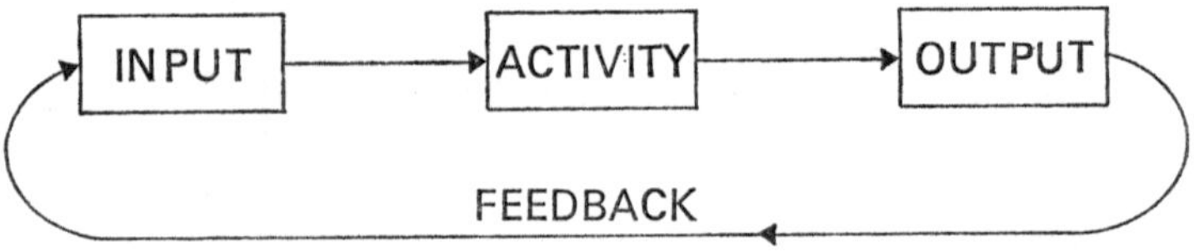

FIG. 4

The model looks at the training process as having three stages. Firstly there is the input into a situation, each piece of input being selected to achieve a defined learning objective. The 'process' is the bringing together of all these inputs and the output is the result of this process. The purpose of the feedback loop is to discover whether or not the output resembles that which was intended when deciding upon the inputs. This is the basis of the evaluation of the fulfilment of learning objectives.

At this point it is necessary to help the reader to start the process of defining what sort of objectives he is seeking in the various learning situations he devises. At a very simple level one might begin with basic medical information. The study of symptoms and signs for example is made so that the practitioner may have knowledge upon which to make decisions. A set of given symptoms and signs indicate the probability of a given disorder. Having decided upon the disorder one then needs recourse to other aspects of knowledge which enable one to make decisions concerning the resolution of that disorder. This sort of information is readily available in medical text-books and articles. Thus a teacher may legitimately elect to refer the learner to such sources. As we will note later on, the way in which he does it offers a wider choice than simply telling him to go and look in a book.

Physical skills may well be described in books, but books are poor media of instruction for learning a physical skill. Even simple tasks like pressing down a tongue with a spatula involves some level of physical skill. It is best learned by the process of demonstration and controlled experience (see Instructing Skills, chapter 7).

The use of knowledge and skills is a much more difficult area to define. The purpose of acquiring such a skill is simply to elicit more knowledge. Depressing the tongue with a spatula is an operation which could be performed by a blacksmith. What distinguishes the blacksmith from the doctor is that the doctor uses his eyes and brain to elicit more clinical information to enhance his existing knowledge, and to use in his decision making.

Perhaps the best way of defining what we mean is to examine the learning required simply to drive a car on the road. It would be possible to instruct a learner on the theoretical practice of driving and the highway code. One could then teach him how to steer a car, how to change gear, how to use the brakes, switch on lights, windscreen wipers, etc. All of this learning, however, cannot guarantee that the learner will then be able to go out on to the road and behave in a proper and safe manner. It becomes necessary at some point to put all the theory, rules and skills together and get out on to the road. This is where one learns to use one's skill and knowledge, because this is where they are both applied.

In our society we choose to do this under the control of a teacher who enables the learner to put his learning into practice and provides feedback on the way in which he is progressing.

In the three areas, 1, 2 and 3 (Morris), we can see that the teacher has a quite important and at times almost dominant role. He is teaching in order that the learner may learn. He is also an active teacher.

When we look at the other three areas, 4, 5 and 6, we come to a situation in which we are obliged to reappraise the role of the teacher. A social skill (4) we would define as the appropriate pattern of behaviour which a person is capable of generating in a social setting. In teaching for example, discussion leading is a social skill. It is possible to define certain traits which are appropriate to that setting and some which are not. A discussion leader should not occupy 99 per cent of the time available for discussion. Unless he is practising 'resource-aided discussion' (see chapter 8) he also ought to be aware of his responsibility to provide support to some members of the group. He ought not to use his privileged position to launch into non-supportive attacks upon the members of his group (unless he really understands the theory of 'conflict teaching', how to use it, when to use it and why he uses it). This sort of skill is very difficult to teach to somebody. One can provide demonstration of how one uses these skills oneself, but one cannot go so far as to claim that one's own model is a perfect prescription. The way in which one man leads a discussion group will be different from the way in which another will lead that group. Despite what many people claim about the innate nature of leadership the evidence suggests that it is a function of a whole group of variables and birth does not figure amongst them (McLeish, 1968).

An interpersonal skill (5) is a refinement of a social skill, appropriate to such a setting such as the one-to-one surgery consultation. Many skills appropriate in larger groups of people are inappropriate here. For example, lecturing is a skill to be used (sparingly) with large audiences. Counselling, however, is best applied in a one-to-one (or maybe a one-to-two setting). We would suggest that a great proportion of the behavioural skills of the doctor are related to this one-to-one setting.

As a teacher one has the task of developing such skills in a student, and one must consider how this should be done. This is where the distinction between teaching and learning on the one hand, and facilitating learning on the other assume real value. There are many learning objectives which the teacher can most efficiently achieve by utilising traditional and well-used teaching techniques, e.g. telling, directed reading, instructing, talking 'at' and talking 'with'. None of these, however, is going to be much use as the primary tool for teaching an individual about his own behaviour patterns. He has got to be able to see and examine his own behaviour patterns for himself. It is no good saying to a trainee, 'I think you handled that patient very badly and you made the wrong diagnosis'. If that is said the trainee will start looking for defences rather than constructive approaches to the situation.

This is where the less directive techniques are so useful, e.g. 'talking at', case studies, role playing, participant observation. All of these situations, as will be seen, are conditioned by the presence of the trainer, but his role is not that of a traditional teacher. As a case-study leader he is continually forcing the trainee to reflect upon his decisions, whilst providing very little of his own views upon the situation. As a role player he might play the doctor or the patient. As we shall see it is his exploration of the role in which the trainee finds himself that is so important.

Finally, self-understanding (6) is one of the most illusive and indefinite of all teaching objectives. Most teachers hope that by using a fair mixture of all techniques they will, as a by-product, induce a lot of self-understanding. In the context of the one-to-one teaching situation, it is probable that the most effective device is counselling. Certainly there is a mass of opinion and research to validate this claim (see recommended reading under Counselling, chapter 11). However, the effectiveness of counselling is dependent upon the effectiveness of the counsellor, and the willingness of the student to be counselled. The sad, and perhaps rather emotional conclusion one comes to about all the caring professions is that the self-understanding of the trainer is possibly the most significant factor in achieving success. Unfortunately teachers and researchers still do not know enough about this area of learning to make quite specific prescriptions.

Chapter 6

THE NATURE OF OBSERVATION (THE PASSIVE ROLE)

One activity of training is the trainee's observation of his trainer at work. There is some evidence that the observation of overt behaviour can be full of learning if, and only if, the learner has learned how to imitate. Miller and Dollard (*op. cit.*) have shown that imitation is a learned behaviour tendency, and have shown that when this tendency is absent then imitative learning does not occur. The trainee may also learn that there are some behaviours which he should not imitate. It is difficult to determine in training how much of the trainer model should be picked up and directly imitated by the trainee. Certainly no reasonable general practitioner would wish to claim that his method of handling patients was a perfect prescription for the rest of his profession. Most general practitioners would be more likely to recognise the fact that each patient coming through his door is a unique person and that good relationships with them are a matter of individual adjustments on the doctor's part rather than the application of some magic formula to make friends and influence people.

Some trainers may well feel that there are certain generalities which can be directly taught to a trainee, and more than one general practitioner has commented upon his own singularly effective approach to the difficult patient. A more likely application to the concept of imitation can be seen when teaching complete techniques such as 'counselling' (chapter 11). As will be noted from that chapter a distinct behavioural pattern can be identified in that particular situation. If we take this as our example we would specify our objective as being:

1. To teach the trainee what behavioural counselling is.
2. To enable him to learn its skills, to internalise them and to use them.
3. To enable him to recognise situations in which counselling should be used.

Counselling, as we have pointed out, is not an activity which can be learned from books. It must ultimately be learned experientially. However, it is quite impossible to learn something experientially unless one knows what to look for in the experience. One approach to this formidable teaching goal would be to start by defining what counselling is.

'. . . that interaction which:

1. occurs between two individuals called a counsellor and a client,
2. takes place in a professional setting, and
3. is initiated and maintained as a means of facilitating changes in the behaviour of the client.'

For a detailed account see chapter 11. Also see Shertzer and Stone (1968).

Having defined what we are talking about we still have not achieved very much. It is also necessary to provide some direct input—even possibly by instruction. One might well wish to move towards a quick appreciation of the stringent rules governing counselling and thus counsellor behaviour. To do this one might begin with a set of rules.

1. Counselling is not the giving of information, although during the process the counsellor may give some information.
2. Counsellors are not givers of advice—open or disguised.
3. Counsellors do not seek to impose their own values, practices or behaviours upon counsellees.
4. Counsellors do not use any disciplinary sanctions to achieve results except such self-discipline which may stem from the counsellee.
5. Counselling is not to be confused with 'interviewing'.

This is a statement of what it is not, and then one would progress on to what it is.

1. Counselling seeks to influence some voluntary behaviour change on the part of the counsellee.
2. Counselling seeks to do this by creating a situation in which the counsellee is able to recognise his own right to determine his own behaviour.
3. The counselling process takes place in face to face, confidential interaction between two people, and one of the important skills is that the counsellor can listen. He must also be able to reflect back to the counsellee what he is saying.

At this point it is well to examine what the trainee might feel. He has now been given a definition of an activity, he has been given rules which prescribe and limit his behaviour within that activity, but apart from what he has assimilated at a cognitive level he is possibly extremely worried. Unless he has had some direct personal experience of counselling he will find it very difficult to know exactly what all this actually means to him.

This then is the point at which we might well consider the introduction of some passive observation. At once difficulties are increased, if only because we believe that counselling is a two-person activity rather than a three-person activity (even if the third person is a passive observer). The problem is to some extent mitigated in general practice because the trainee is likely to be an accepted addition to the normal surgery situation. If the trainer considers it advisable it is obviously much more effective from the trainee's point of view to see the whole counselling situation for real. However, we recognise that on occasion substitutes for reality may well have to be used, e.g. cassette recorders or V.T.R.

Having observed some counselling for real the trainee is then in a position to commence to discuss this activity with his trainer, for he is now beginning to acquire greater insights into the situation. Having been present and having seen the process he will also have some emotional experience of what it is like to be in such a situation and this is possibly more important at this stage than any factual learning which he may have derived.

Considerable and rapid development is now possible. The trainee, if he can imitate, may well like to experiment with the trainer simply to find out if he has got the feel of the reflecting technique for example.

As we pointed out when we looked at instructional skills, the seeing of the total activity being demonstrated by another can be of some considerable value. However, one must add riders. It is pointless planting a trainee (or medical student) in a corner of the surgery and telling him to become a mute decoration for a whole day. We cannot stress enough the importance of utilising the period immediately following a consultation, even for one minute or so, to make sure that the trainee has the opportunity to ask any question which is bothering him, or for his trainer to focus his attention on something which he considers important.

CHAPTER 7

INSTRUCTING SKILLS

Most people conceive of the teacher as someone who spends his time instructing others. It is unlikely that many of those for whom this book has been prepared have had the opportunity to experience at first hand the revolution in teaching methods which has so fundamentally changed primary education and some parts of the secondary system. It is also unlikely that they will have had experience of certain types of management education which, for adults, is probably the area of greatest innovation in education today.

For most of us our best remembered teacher will have been a Mr Chips, while perhaps our worst may have been a Mr Squeers. Most of us, however, have had experience of one teacher somewhere in our educational experience, who because of his enthusiasm for his discipline, or his genuine concern for his charges, has stood for us above other teachers as a symbol of 'good' teaching.

As it is probable that we have also modelled our own teaching performance upon such a one or upon an unconscious composite of the various teacher roles with which we have been in contact, it is for each of us teachers worth considering just how we have arrived at our own personal style. We may then obtain some insight into our private beliefs about the act of teaching. As few of us have in fact sought such insight into these beliefs it is worth considering in this section on instructional skills what they may be.

If our self-view shows us a teacher who spends most of his time 'talking at' other people, or conducting tightly controlled discussions one must ask the questions, 'Do I really think that in my teaching situations the learner has anything to offer? Is he a passive member of this smallest group, or should he be an active member?' It is quite easy to rationalise the learner's response to a single directed question as involvement, whereas it may well indicate nothing more than the fact that he is awake.

Perhaps the most difficult technique of all when instructing others is that of judging the appropriate level of learner participation. Before beginning the process of instruction one normally thinks about what one is going to say, then plans the way in which one intends to say it, asking the questions, 'Does the learner really need to know all this, or does he already know all this?' There are points in all attachment situations at which the teacher, however participative he may be, finds himself in a situation where he has a considerable body of information and opinion which the learner does not have. Then the problem is, simply, how does the teacher put this information over to the student?

Let us begin by saying that most of the methods most of us have experienced when we were obliged to assimilate a lot of information are not appropriate to the 'one-to-one' learning situation. It would be a bizarre experience if a teacher were to stand at a rostrum and deliver a one-hour lecture to one student. It might even be worse if the teacher were to prepare eight foolscap pages of notes and then read them to the student. It is easy to see that the exhibition of such extreme behaviour would indicate little or no insight on the teacher's part, but in the lesser situation of a five minutes 'one-to-one' lecture or a half-page of notes read, many are guilty of just this type of behaviour.

This does not mean that there is no place for straightforward didactic instruction in the attachment situation. What it does mean is that if the teacher finds himself in a situation where other than didactic instructional skills are required then he must think a little about how the situation is to be managed.

One way of handling it is to split the situation into two portions. The first and by far the easiest, is when one is faced with the problem of teaching a simple physical skill. In the surgery there may well be a piece of equipment such as a Vitallograph with which the trainee is not familiar. It is possible to use 'discovery methods' (including an instruction sheet!) which will allow the student to find out how it works, but a straightforward approach involving direct teaching will also serve. This type of teaching activity has been written about by innumerable writers, but most appear to agree that there is a series of rules and steps which together create an efficient sequential learning experience.

Step 1 *Prepare yourself.* Be clear about what it is that you want to impart, go through the operation as you normally would, only attempting, where possible, to break the operation down into a series of self-contained steps. Examine your sequence of operations and decide how you will explain each one of these. In fact all that is required is that one plans what one is going to do.

Step 2 *Prepare the trainee.* Begin by making absolutely clear to him what it is that you are going to show him. In doing this you make sure that he does not know already what you are proposing to teach. Explain to him what the instrument does and how it is of assistance in one's work. Let the trainee stand beside you so that he sees the job done with as near to the same view as he would have had were he doing it himself. Do not let him stand opposite because he might then obtain an incorrect 'mirror' view of the task. Give one or two complete demonstrations at a normal speed of operation.

Step 3 *Present the job step by step.* This is where preparation pays off. Each step of the operation which the trainee sees is presented as it were in slow motion. These steps are then presented individually and each of them is explained. Allow the trainee to ask as many questions as he may wish and, in passing, to handle for himself the piece of equipment. Allow plenty of time.

Step 4 *Allow the trainee to try out each step for himself, giving the appropriate feedback as to his performance.* Then allow him to attempt to put all the operations together into sequence. Finally get him to explain to you how the job is done.

Step 5 *Allow him to use the equipment on his own.* There is a great temptation at this point to cluck like a mother hen in approval or disapproval whilst the trainee performs this activity. Whilst some teachers would not agree, there is a lot to be said for allowing him to make mistakes and then allowing him to discover that he has made mistakes. Perhaps a more helpful ploy at this stage is simply to be there, but to have made clear that you, the teacher, are a resource for the trainee and will provide help for him if he requires it. Some industrial trainers who are aware of the problems involved in learning physical skills have a rule which goes something like, 'unless he is going to wreck the machine let him make all the mistakes he needs to make in order to learn the task. Where possible try to make sure he does not lose too many fingers in the process.' This apparently crude and light-hearted rule contains an aliphatic dose of common sense.

It should be noted here that some teachers do not believe that learners should be allowed to make mistakes. The more one discusses this issue with these teachers the more one comes to the conclusion that they are not supporting a particular school of psychological enquiry but a deep-seated belief about 'the self' as a teacher. In making their statement the authors of this work have taken their own stand and have thus revealed something about their own personalities.

The teaching of a physical skill(s) relating to an instrument or to a piece of equipment is one matter, but without such a material peg upon which to hang the lesson, there can be thorny problems.

When faced with the situation of presenting information which cannot be tied to a piece of equipment the situation becomes more difficult. There is always a great temptation for the teacher actually to start 'teaching' at this point. So many teachers develop a series of 'pet lectures' which they can draw out of the hat as soon as any likely occasion presents itself. So many teachers also know that simply to blast information at a learner is about the least effective method of facilitating his learning. McLeish (1968) demonstrates that only about 6 per cent of the total material presented in such a situation is retained. This figure does not seem to be markedly affected whether the learner makes notes or not. Thus our position would be summed up by offering as a basic proposition for all teachers—when you find you have been speaking for more than ten minutes you have been talking for too long.

What constitutes information is perhaps the most difficult of all questions to answer. There is information which is factual, and can be ascertained by reference to empirically derived research. There is information which is largely opinion. Most of us at several stages in our progress through whatever passed for our 'education' have suffered gravely when 'experts' have presented opinion in the guise of factual information using the vehicle of a straight lecture. There comes a point in all such lectures where something said by the lecturer starts a mental process which continues in our heads and we stop listening to what the lecturer is saying. Utter frustration occurs at the point when we assemble all the 'information' which could refute his 'information' only to find that neither is the opportunity offered to interject, nor is what we wish to interject appropriate to what the lecturer is talking about by the time we have marshalled our ideas.

Hence we feel that we need to stress again the point about preparation. Part of our preparation should be concerned to ascertain whether or not the subject matter is opinion or hard provable information. If there is the slightest doubt that one is dealing with material which might be classified as factual information then one must construct a teaching situation which allows maximum time for student involvement and participation.

If we take as an example the teaching a general practitioner trainer must at some stage undertake with his trainee concerning the financing of a practice we may then examine the various nuances which can colour one's dealings with a matter which is apparently wholly factual.

The financing of a practice is to some extent dependent upon statutes and written regulations. A statute itself is a most difficult thing to define. The words of any statute can be read by any literate person, but if there was no vagueness about them there would also be many fewer lawyers than there are.

The regulations themselves offer every practice a whole range of options, some of which may be limited by various factors inherent in the practice or its environment but they, with others, offer every practice a considerable range of choice. The actual combination of options used in any one practice could never be described as the perfect prescription for all practices, but there may well be an optimisation of choices open to a variety of practices. Every trainer wishing to explore this area with his trainee will also doubtless hold personal opinions about his own selection of options.

Our trainer then has decided to explore this area with his trainee. Unlike instruction into the mysteries of the Vitallograph (where the trainee either knows or does not know how to use it) it is possible that the trainee will already have some ideas as to how a practice ought to be financed. Thus in this case an essential part of the trainer's self-preparation will be to discover what the trainee knows, or thinks he knows, before they start.

Based upon his identification of the trainee's deficiencies of knowledge the trainer can then move to a second stage where he will be able to advise the trainee which of the multitude of Department of Health and Social Security publications he needs to read to obtain the 'facts' upon which some options may be based.

In the third stage he must be concerned to examine how much more the trainee feels he has learned as a result of his reading. Even though it is of vital importance to a trainee to know and to understand how a practice ought to be financed, most of the relevant literature is extraordinarily dull and uninspiring. There is thus a distinct likelihood that the trainee will not have read all that he should have read.

Having achieved a basic input the trainer can then go on to explain how he has chosen to finance his own practice. At this point a wide variety of training approaches are open. For example, the trainer may opt simply to tell the trainee how he does it, or he may seek to offer the trainee a set of D.H. & S.S. options and allow him to make his own choice. This would be followed by an examination of the choice and, where possible, its implications. Alternatively the trainer may prepare a written sheet which explains how he has financed his own practice and then set the trainee the task of examining him in how and why he came to make the options. Yet another alternative might be to invite the trainee to 'discover' which options the trainer has chosen simply by examining the workings of the practice.

These various options have become more and more open-ended as they were developed. The point to bear in mind is that there is no perfect prescription for an approach to teaching anything. The approach is a function of the material, the teacher and the learner. This book, or for that matter hundreds of similar books, cannot permutate all the possible variations which might occur. Here, perhaps, is the greatest limitation suffered by those who wish to write books on educational methodology.

The management of the 'tell and talk' approach is much easier than that obtaining when a trainee is let loose to 'discover' for himself. Some trainees may never be sufficiently motivated to wish to discover the mechanisms of practice finance—and thus will be much happier with 'tell and talk', or even with caring for patients. Other trainees might well see finance as the most vital part of their existence and would thus respond much better to a more exploratory situation. There is also the possibility that some trainers do not really know how their own practices are financed and are therefore quite unable to 'tell'. They may learn something by letting the trainee find out for himself. He would then 'tell' them how they do it.

This chapter is not, however, the most important component of this book. Most active professional people have had sufficient life experience to be able to instruct adequately, while our main purpose is to help trainers to look at other than the traditional approaches to teaching. It must be said that there will inevitably be many occasions upon which there is a fundamental disparity of information between the trainer and the trainee, and such situations may well lend themselves to formal teaching approaches. As long as the teacher is continually making sure that the learner is learning then formal teaching or 'telling' has an important place in our armoury of teaching methods. The gravest sin that a teacher may commit in this or indeed any sort of situation is to teach and then not check that what has been taught has also been learned.

Chapter 8

'TALKING AT', 'TALKING WITH' AND 'BEING TALKED TO'

When we consider 'discussion' in the educational sense it is usual to present it as an activity which takes place somewhere in a spectrum progressing from leader-centred discussion through group-centred discussion into resource-aided discussion. The appended sociograms will illustrate the differences. In the group models arrows indicate communications to and from people. In the one-to-one models the thickness of the arrow indicates the volume of contribution made by one or other of the individuals concerned.

Leader-centred discussion

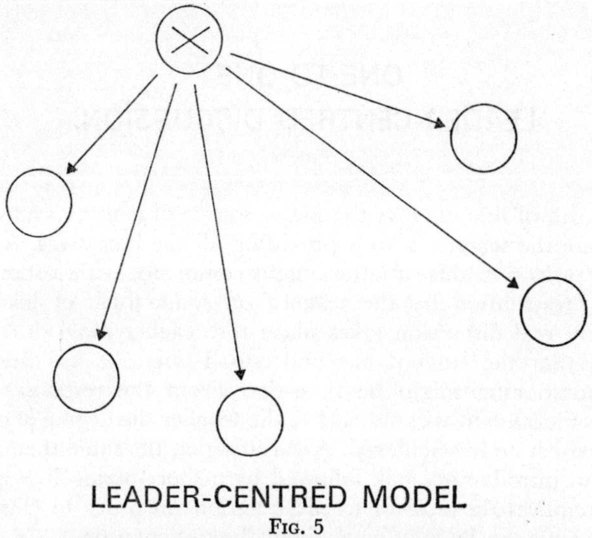

LEADER-CENTRED MODEL

Fig. 5

(The circle containing the X indicates the teacher)

Clearly in this type of discussion there is not an interaction between six people, but five separate conversations between six people, for there is but one focus of attention—the teacher (or leader). Some teachers consider this to be not a discussion but a directively structured talk. Every situation, however, must be looked at from the point of view of its learning utility. What can be done in this situation to enhance effective learning? One obvious conclusion is that, if an introductory talk is to be given in this situation, the teacher justifiably will wish to know if the content of his talk has been understood. He may simply do this by allowing individual members of the group to ask him questions. Thence he may discern both areas of vagueness and misperceptions. He may also use this situation to determine, by asking questions himself whether or not the various points he has been making have been comprehended.

Yet if we are dealing with only two people the above sociogram will not suffice, so that we redraw it in a different way which demonstrates the similarity. In fact the sociograms of groups are built up from those of the smallest group—of two people.

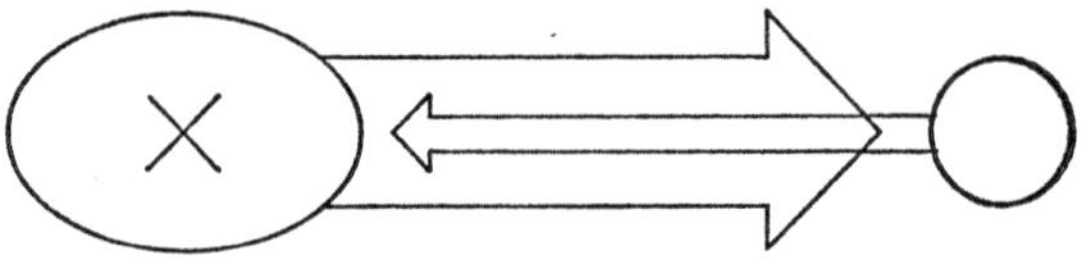

ONE-TO-ONE
LEADER-CENTRED DISCUSSION

Fig. 6

The breadth of line denotes the major source of activity and control, in this case the teacher who is providing all the initiatives. A typical teaching process in this situation might commence with a short introductory presentation by the teacher on some topic of his choice. Before any real discussion takes place the teacher may also wish to ascertain that the student has understood what he has been told. Hence questioning might be in order. From the responses to the questions the student will indicate to the teacher the degree of comprehension which he has achieved. A variation on the same theme might well be an introductory talk followed by a short period in which the teacher requires the student to ask questions in order to clarify any areas of vagueness he may have about the presentation.

The important feature of this kind of interaction is that the teacher has complete control over the content of the discussion, its direction and its purpose. The most likely teaching purpose therefore in this teaching/learning situation will be 'teaching that' with only a small admixture of 'teaching to'.

Group-centred discussion

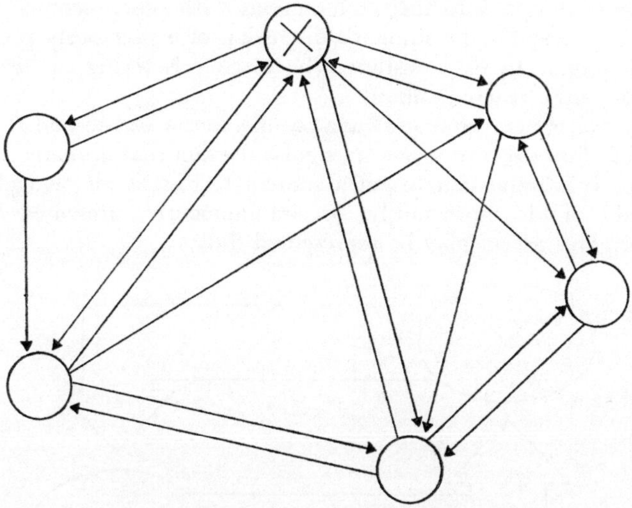

GROUP-CENTRED DISCUSSION

FIG. 7

In this type of 'classic discussion' the teacher has changed his status from that of pure 'teacher' to that of 'teacher member' of a group. It is still the teacher who determines what the group will talk about, but now he is prepared to allow the group itself to decide how it will manage its discussion. His role is largely that of an informed group member who occasionally exercises also the role of chairman. His prime purpose, however, is to allow group members to interact with each other—and he is seeking to use the group to bring members to consider various normative positions which may occur in the group context.

An important consideration in this setting is that the teacher in his chosen role has opted to occupy less of the talking time available to the group. Whereas in the leader-centred group he might occupy more than half of the time available, in this type of group he accepts the fact that he only has a right to one-sixth. He has ceded to the group much of his power of initiation and to a lesser extent of direction. He still has, however, his objectives and still seeks to pursue them.

This sort of discussion is useful when one is seeking to encourage students to consider how they might be able to use knowledge or ideas which they have learned. It is also a situation in which people may gain some insight into their interactions with other people. It is a useful variation for the student's discussion of a previously presented written paper. In each instance the teacher is trying to 'teach to' probably after 'teaching about'.

This type of discussion also has a parallel in the 'one-to-one' relationship in so far as it is proper to recognise the fact that in many areas of learning it is important to get a student to discuss his own ideas in the light of ideas previously, or simultaneously, presented by his teacher. This aspect may be represented thus:

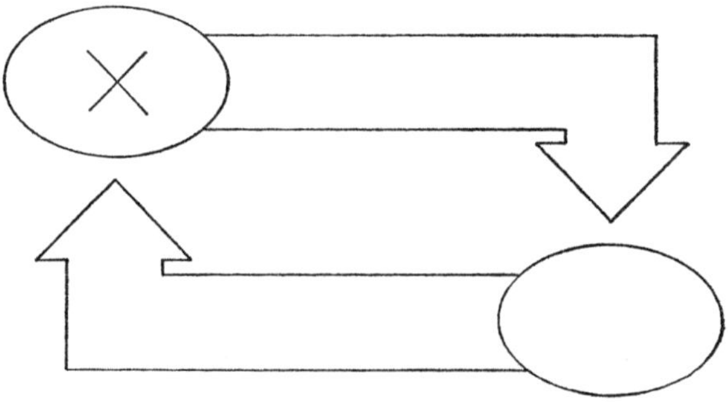

ONE-TO-ONE
GROUP CENTRED
FIG. 8

A study of the way Socrates taught 3000 years ago demonstrates the 'classic' discussion, a method which properly used is still supreme.

A third type of discussion model which can be isolated is that referred to by educationists as the:

Resource-aided discussion group

Here the teacher is not an effective member of the group, and moreover he is physically and constitutionally outside the group setting. He functions solely as a resource to the group. He will, if so requested, aid the group when it requires information or opinion (factual resource), but he will also step in should he perceive that the group has major problems of constitutionality (leadership resource). Otherwise he will remain quite outside the situation.

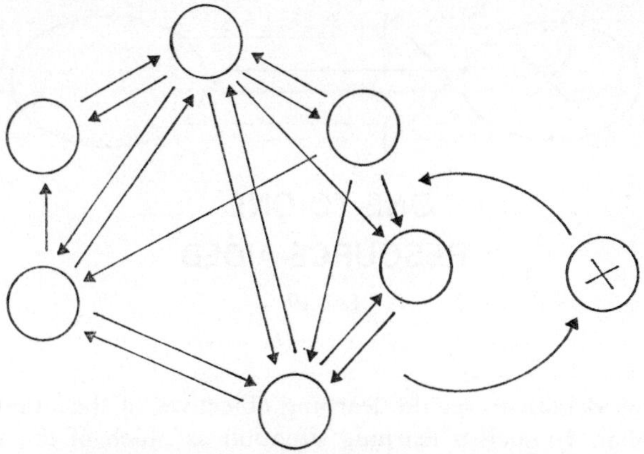

RESOURCE-AIDED DISCUSSION

FIG. 9

While it is still possible that the teacher has decided what the group is going to talk about, it is unlikely that he will have given it any input. In this sort of situation the purposes would be that the group not only works at a central theme and seeks to achieve normative conslusions, but that the group also pays attention to the way in which it is organising itself and managing its task.

An enormous amount of social learning is believed to be possible in these situations. In the terms we have already offered this type of group is nearly always concerned with 'teaching to'. The most obvious feature of such a group is that the teacher is not actually doing any 'teaching'. He does not occupy any power position within the group, but rather a reference point outside it. He is in many ways a mirror, reflecting back at the group what he perceives to be their values and practices.

Later on we shall be discussing non-directive counselling and this technique has distinct utility in this group situation. If we are looking for direct anologies we might well conceive a situation in which the teacher implicitly says to the student, 'Now you teach me about so and so.' Thus, in terms of our models, we would achieve a reversal of the first model.

In this situation the initiatives and control lie with the student. At the discussion level the teacher might want to join in and discuss the task or content of the teaching. He might usefully also look upon this relationship as a way in which he can get substantial feedback upon the effect his teaching has had upon the student. In this type of learning situation perjorative statements by the teacher are inappropriate. This is largely the area of 'teaching to' where the student has

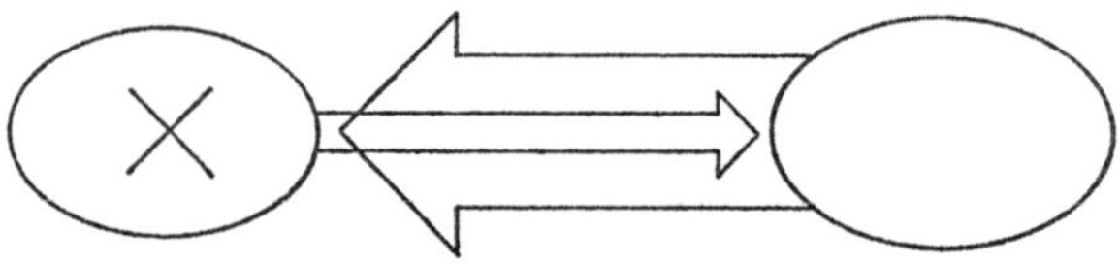

ONE-TO-ONE
RESOURCE-AIDED

FIG. 10

been allowed both to set the learning objectives of the situation and to control it. In such a learning situation as much of the student's material (content) may revolve around normative material, it is unwise for the teacher directly to challenge the validity of the student's content. If a student says, 'This is what I believe . . .' and his statement is followed by a response from the teacher which begins, 'What you believe is quite wrong, or immoral . . .', then the chances of the teacher being able to modify the student's initial belief are limited because the student will predictably jump to a defence of his own position. If the teacher is concerned about the student's statement a more appropriate response might be, 'Would you like to examine the implications of what you have just said?'

It may reasonably be asked at this point why these various group situations have not been termed 'seminars' or 'tutorials'. Unfortunately there is so little agreement on what they mean by the terms amongst those who provide seminars and tutorials that no meaningful distinctions exist. What is important is to recognise that many teachers operate what they call tutorials or seminars from the rigid base of a personal model without having thought about that model as it applies to their own learning objectives. They thus tend to conduct a uniform series of sessions regardless of the desired learning outcome. These face-to-face settings do have the in-built potential for a considerable degree of flexibility in their form, while pragmatically, one may observe that different forms appear to achieve different learning objectives. There is so little hard research evidence to confirm these observations that until such is available we are forced to rely upon subjective rather than upon objective judgements.

Although this is a short section it probably deals with the most common of all teaching/learning methods used in the attachment. What we have tried to emphasise is the fact that by amending the role-relationship of trainer and trainee different sorts of learning may be pursued.

CHAPTER 9

NON-DIRECTIVE TEACHING

It is worth repeating that the existence and use of non-directive teaching methods does not mean the absence of learning objectives. It does, however, mean the absence of an authoritarian approach to the learning situation. Some of the methods which we have already examined are in fact, if properly used, non-directive. If, for example, we consider a case-study, spelling out the details of the case as presented by the trainer, who then says to the trainee, 'What would you do now?', as long as the trainer is not keeping some 'perfect solution' up his sleeve and is prepared to accept the fact that each human situation will be differently approached by different people, then one is using non-directive methodology. The case-study becomes a directive procedure when the trainer presents all the data and then goes on to present a perfect solution. It is difficult to evaluate the outcome of the directive study because it will depend upon how frequently 'the perfect solution' occurs. If we accept that one purpose of the attachment situation is to train people how to work with other people, then it is unlikely that 'perfect solutions' will be common. In real-life circumstances the directive, or more correctly termed 'closed ended' method can only hope to teach general principles.

On the other hand if one were considering asking a trainee to role-play an interaction with a patient before actually letting him loose on real patients one would be doing so to gain some insight into the way in which he might behave in a similar real-life situation. It is the way in which the analysis of such a situation is handled that is critical. If, after the trainee has role-played an interview, the trainer comes to the conclusion that the trainee had made a complete mess of it, the trainer is faced with a choice of actually saying to the trainee, 'Well, that was a complete shambles, wasn't it?' or he can try to get the trainee to examine his own behaviour pattern.

Clearly here is an area where there will be a wide range of opinion about a particular situation. For example, if a student role-playing an interaction arrives at the correct diagnosis whilst at the same time managing to irritate the patient, has he succeeded? The answer may depend upon the individual trainer's view of the purpose and conditions of general practice. It is also quite possible that the trainee achieves a first-class human relationship whilst arriving at the wrong diagnosis.

What is important in *both case-studies and role-playing* is that the trainer should realise that they are not teaching methods which allow him to impose his own personality all over the trainee. They are methods which seek to allow a trainee to examine his *own* reactions in a given situation, in order that he will be aware of how he behaves and to discover what effect his behaviour has upon others.

When subjected to a straightforward critical appraisal of our own behaviour we normally react by attempting to find a set of defences to protect something which we might not wish to defend. We are more likely to consider our own behaviour more closely if we are in a situation in which outsiders are apparently not making any judgements on us but are seen to be helping us to make our own judgements.

If the above assertions are generally true then there are great problems for the trainer who knows that in a particular situation the trainee's behaviour was wrong, or inappropriate.

The next section of this book is concerned primarily with non-directive or, as it is sometimes known, 'behavioural' counselling. Non-directive counselling is possibly the most valuable technique for making a learner examine his own ideas, feelings, assumptions and behaviours. It is a difficult teaching technique for general practitioners to learn, simply because having clear uses in therapeutic medicine, its educational uses to which we confine ourselves are not readily apparent.

Before commencing such an analysis it is important to clarify the 'teacher styles' most commonly associated with non-directive teaching.

We must begin with a clear redefinition of the role of a teacher. The non-directive teacher is concerned to ensure that the student makes 'discoveries' for himself rather than to have 'discoveries' made for him. His concern will be to devise situations within which he feels that the student can make discoveries. Thus the teacher is always aware of in which area he would like the student to learn and indeed is often aware of what he would like the student to learn. Although there are genuine doubts as to whether or not this is the best way to teach a child that two plus two equals four, there can be few doubts as to its utility in assisting a student to learn about his own behaviour.

The distinction being drawn is that between 'teaching' and 'learning'. Some teachers spend their time 'teaching', others spend their time 'encouraging others to learn'. One does not have actually to tell a student something in order that he may learn it. One suspects that many of the teachers who 'tell' students do so in order to be able to say to themselves, 'I have told'. Non-directive teaching is a form of teaching in which the teacher spends only little of his time teaching in the form of 'telling'. If we take the example of properly used role-playing the teacher does not first spell out the situation, then the characteristics of each member of the drama, and then behave like a film director. Once he has created the scene and provided the backdrop he has no further part in that transaction until the play has been acted out. At that point he may, under certain circumstances, become a 'teller'.

This approach to teaching then requires its own form of discipline. It presupposes in the learner both a desire to learn and the existence of a high degree of self-discipline. More important, however, is the discipline it imposes upon the teacher. He must ever resist the temptation to rush into situations to start providing his own interpretations and solutions. He must recognise that in the field of interpersonal relations his own reactions are unique and may well be wholly unsuitable as a pattern upon which the student should model himself.

Mouly (1968) (summarising work by Burton) outlines the major points of contrast which exist when comparing two different approaches to education.

SUBJECT MATTER UNITS	EXPERIENCE UNITS
Begin in the intention of teachers, to teach approved subject matter to students;	*Begin* in the intention of the learner, to achieve some purpose; to satisfy some need;
are organised logically around a core within the subject matter;	are organised psychologically around a purpose of the learner;
are prepared in advance by a person or group already familiar with materials and their logic;	are organised as they develop by a group facing a new situation for the first time;
are for the purpose of having the learner acquire the logically arranged subject matter;	are for the immediate purpose of satisfying needs of the learner, and with the ultimate purpose of developing desirable understandings, attitudes, skills in the learner;
are usually organised from simple to complex within subject area fields;	are usually organised functionally and in disregard of subject lines;
are controlled by teachers, some outside agency and by the course of study;	are controlled by co-operating group of learners, which includes the teacher; the course of study is utilised as needed;

are usually centred in the past, in the accumulated culture and not in the accumulating culture; little reference to present or future; reference to future often theoretical;	are usually centred in present or future: use accumulated material from the past freely in solving present problems;
rely on formal methods, assignments distinct lesson types, printed material as chief sources, learning experiences few and formal;	utilise co-operatively planned procedures suited to the situation: sources in great variety, learning experiences numerous and varied;
give all learners the same contact with the same materials; some provision for individual differences;	give contacts with many materials individual differences cared for variously and automatically;
have fixed outcomes, known in advance and required uniformly for all learners;	do not have fixed outcomes which are known in advance and required uniformly for all learners;
at conclusion, evaluate through use of formal tests of subject matter acquisition, usually of fact or skill;	evaluate many complex outcomes continually, with constant pupil participation and through the use of many instruments, formal and informal;
close with a backward look, so-called review, and are done with when finished.	lead to new interests, problems and purposes.

Whereas the differences in the two approaches involve many facets that deny easy synthesis, the major differences lies in their orientation. In fact they are predicted upon relatively incompatible assumptions.

It is clearly not helpful to part-time trainers to involve them in the complicated academic debates over approaches to learning and the basic philosophies underlying each particular school. Every argument has some validity and none have a monopoly of truth. A compromise position might be found by accepting those truths from each side which suit one's own particular approach to the teaching/learning situation. Although the writers of this book are more likely to support the experiential approach, the very fact that they have written a book indicates that they also have some weakness for the subject matter approach.

It is unlikely that many of the present generation of trainers will have had first-hand experience of anything other than a subject matter approach to the learning situation. Over the last six years there have been a series of experimental courses at Manchester designed to 'teach' general practitioners the technique *inter alia* of counselling, utilising almost exclusively the experiential approach. The results of these experiments are now being researched in various ways, but what we seem to have learnt is that the course members, to one degree or another, 'know' that they have been exposed to a learning technique which for most of them has been quite new. It is also initially traumatic, but subsequently, once they learn the new rules, the greatest teaching problem is to moderate the euphoria at the end of the course.

In order to move into 'less directive' teaching situations it is necessary to move at one's own pace through the various techniques offered here. If trainers find that they are happy with the situation in which they find themselves and are gaining the sort of results which they value then they may well be encouraged to proceed. What we also must admit is that some teachers are more at home with subject matter approaches and as that approach has sustained education for at least 3000 years it cannot be all bad.

The distinctions between the 'subject matter' and 'experiential' approaches are of particular importance when applied to our example of the caring professions—to general practice. Patients are involved and the doctor's understanding, relationships and management are all important. So is the patient. The knowledge that general practice is not composed of traditional clinical medicine alone, presents the trainer at once with the difficulty that concern for the patient must be seen by the trainee to be as important as concern for good organic medicine. The learning of organic medicine may well be susceptible to straightforward instruction towards an established set of predetermined goals. This type of education has a clear advantage that its results may be easily measured.

Learning to recognise symptoms and to select appropriate treatments involves degrees of judgement. However, the discovery that a patient with recognised symptoms will not accept the selected treatment involves a range of problem solving which cannot be dealt with by conventional educational input. Unless one can reduce the management of difficult patients to simple generalisations it is not, at first glance, easy to see how one provides the learning necessary to be able to handle them.

At one of our recent courses for trainees we found that they were very short of responses when confronted with the problem of the 'difficult' patient. Their competence in dealing with disease was of a high order, but their ability to distinguish between 'the presented' and 'the real' problem of the patient was not. Several of them went so far as to claim that they saw treatment of 'presented' problems as the limit of their responsibility as a general practitioner.

Were this an acceptable approach to general practice then they would be correct in their statement. But general practice is all about 'whole person medicine' and so this narrow viewpoint must be widened.

An analysis of the following doctor/patient consultation offers some insight into the possible depths which can exist in a consultation and it goes far beyond the treatment of the presented problems. This consultation was recorded on audiotape with the patient's knowledge and permission. (The authors are indebted to Dr C. M. Harris for providing this material.)

D: 'Come in . . . Good morning . . . Sorry to keep you waiting Mrs M . . . These are two medical students.'
M: 'I presumed so.'
D: 'That's O.K.?'
M: 'Yes.'
D: 'Please sit down.'
M: 'After seven children I've seen a lot of them.'
D: 'A lot of medical students?'
M: 'Yes.'
D: 'So what can I do for you?'

Up to this point Mrs M has been bright and has enveloped some of her responses in laughter, especially the one concerning the number of medical students she has seen.

M: 'To be quite honest I don't know. I just feel awful. I keep going hot and cold. My eyes come up. I'm nearly 45 and I suppose I must be on the change now?'
D: 'What shall I tell you now?'
M: (Laughter.) 'No . . . Women have done it before.'
D: 'Is that what you are telling yourself?'
M: 'That's what I'm presuming . . . I don't know.'
D: 'Mmm Mmm' (agreement noises). 'What does the change mean to you?'
M: 'I don't know. But my periods are some months heavy . . . some months I have two.'
D: 'Mmm Mmm.'
M: 'Last month I had two and the one now was due last Friday.'

D: 'Mmm Mmm. What does the change mean as an idea to you? I mean . . .'

M: 'Well, I don't know. I have an idea that it is usual for women. They have these hot flushes, and they don't feel for this and they don't feel for that . . . but my mother used to have blackouts.'

D: 'When she was on the change you mean?'

M: 'Yes.'

D: 'Mmm. And you are worried you would be . . .'

M: 'Well, I don't know . . . but I'm frightened.'

D: 'Mmm Mmm. Frightened of what?'

M: 'Of getting blackouts, or anything like that.' (Voice level drops.)

D: 'You are frightened of more than blackouts?'

M: (Nervous laugh.) 'Well it's not that I choose to. We used to find her miles away on buses.'

Short silence. Mrs M has started to cry.

D: 'Go on.'

M: (Crying openly.) 'Well she never knew how she got there.'

D: 'Mmm Mmm. And that was supposed to be due to the change?'

M: 'Well, that's what she told me. I don't know.'

D: 'And when did she tell you that?'

M: (Continues crying for a few seconds.) 'Well, it's years ago. She's dead now. I think she was going out of her mind. Well, it's years ago . . . twenty-three years ago.'

D: 'Mmm Mmm.'

M: 'Well, she used to go out on the bus. Then they'd find her miles away. And she never knew how. I never knew, but my father used to say she was "on the change".'

D: 'So for the last twenty years you have thought of the change as a time when you . . .?

M: 'Well, I have really.'

D: 'So when you get to forty-five and your periods get irregular . . .'

M: 'Well, you think. Well, you do get worried . . . I suppose. I don't know.'

D: 'But you know, because you've seen in the past twenty years other women get past the age of change without going the way your mother went? So does that mean you feel more like her than . . .?'

M: 'Well, you know, are these things inherited—that's what I want to know? That's what worried me.

D: 'Did she keep on doing it for years, or was it just for a short space in time?'

M: 'Well, no. I think it went on for a couple of years, and then she used to have these blackouts . . . and she used to haemorrhage from the nose.

D: Mmm.

M: And she used to go unconscious. And she had a baby when she was forty-one. And I remember them saying at the time that she would probably be all right then. But as far as I remember she was worse.

D: 'After having the baby?'

M: 'Yes.'

D: 'Well, do you feel that these things which happened to her were connected with having a baby at forty-one?'

M: 'Well, I don't know. People say that if you have a baby on the turn then you are all right.

D: 'What kind of treatment did she have when she was doing this?'

M: 'Well, she didn't really. She was old-fashioned. She wouldn't go anywhere. She wouldn't go to the doctor, and she wouldn't go to the hospital. She did eventually. We insisted, and they found nothing wrong with her. She had . . . what did she have . . . this brain test?'

D: 'An E.E.G.?'

M: 'Mmm Mmm. She had that and they didn't find anything. She was very heavy and they said she had to cut her weight down, but she didn't.'

D: 'Mmm Mmm.'

M: But she just carried on and then she just died suddenly. She was fifty-nine . . . Of heart failure and bronchitis.'

D: 'Is that on your mind as well?'

M: 'No, not really. I don't think about that. It's just that I think about this . . . um um . . . change. God help I don't go like her.'

D: 'Do you have any sisters?'

M: 'Mmm Mmm.'

D: 'Are they older than you or younger?'

M: 'They are younger.'

D: 'Have they got the same kind of fears about the change as you?'

M: 'I don't know. I've never asked them. One's twenty-eight, and the other's thirty-six.'

D: 'So you are a good bit older than them?'

M: 'Yes. I can remember, they can't.'

D: 'There perhaps was a time when you were almost as much their mother as your mother was?'

M: 'Well, it could be. Well, I almost brought the others up, you know.'

D: 'Are you a motherly person?'

M: 'Well, I've got seven of my own.' (She has stopped crying and is now beginning to laugh again.) 'So I am . . . Yes.'

D: 'Have you talked to anybody or your husband about this yet?'

M: 'No, I haven't.'

D: 'So you've bottled it all up. And now it just won't stay bottled any more.'

M: (Crying again.) 'No, but it's silly . . . Nobody ever asked me before, before you asked me. And I know it's there when I think about it.'

D: 'When you came here today had you intended to tell me this?'

M: 'No.'

D: 'How come you did tell me then?'

M: 'I suppose I didn't try really . . . you don't.' (Crying again.) 'I don't know. It's something you don't talk about. If you did someone would say you were daft. I suppose it's inside you really. I've had a very happy life, my mother didn't. Fair enough. Whether that had anything to do with it, I don't know.'

D: 'You have had a happy married life?'

M: 'Well, I have done. My mother didn't. My father used to knock her about. The usual story, you know. Whether that had anything to do with it I don't know.

D: 'Why do you think your husband would think you were daft if you were to tell him?'

M: 'Well, he's very sensible. He says these things don't happen and he'd go on as though it were all right. I don't know. I'm just saying this.'

D: 'But if he could see how important it was to you . . . do you think he would react like that?'

M: 'Well, if he knew how important it was . . . well . . . well . . . it was him who made me come here. He said, "Why don't you go and see the doctor, you keep putting it off and putting it off, and saying it's the change, it could be anything." ' (Mrs M still showing signs of distress.)

D: 'Do you feel any different now, from when you came in?'

M: 'I don't know. It's a silly thing. You have seven children and you do this and do that. You've got to get it behind yourself. You pretend it's not there, but it's there all the time. And you keep thinking to yourself, well it might be all right. I've been happily married, why worry?'

D: 'So today you've done something very different from what you normally do?'

M: I have, yes. I never expected it.

D: 'Right. I think that's very good. I'd like you to come back and see me next week.'

M: (Still crying.) 'Is it the change?'

D: 'If your periods have been going irregular then it may be. Sure.'

M: 'Well, I've always been regular, let's face it . . . as far as these things go. Now it goes that I have none this month and then next month I have two.'

D: 'O.K. We can go into those sort of details next week. But, I think you've done something very big this week. I don't want to start confusing you now with all sorts of little details.'

The interview, which occupied $7\frac{1}{4}$ minutes, finished at this point. The next interview with this patient, a week later, was concerned not with her menopausal problems but with her now-discovered real problems at home with her husband. Each consultation took place within a scheduled morning surgery, although when medical students are present, the time per patient is longer than normal.

The only clue the doctor had in this situation was that the patient, even though she was laughing, showed a slight twitching in the corner of her mouth. He suspected this to mean that she was close to tears and hence chose to avoid here all presenting noises and probe a little deeper. He might, legitimately perhaps, have merely prescribed for her a tranquilliser.

Now let us examine how the trainer managed the learning situation as soon as the patient had left. The trainee was the first to speak.

Trainee: 'How did you know?'

Trainer: 'Did you notice anything strange about her behaviour when she started?'

(Note: The trainer 'knows' what he wants to extract from the situation, i.e. the non-verbal cues. However, he resisted the temptation 'to tell' and has pushed the problem back to the trainee.)

Trainee: 'Well . . . I noticed that she was rather nervous.'

Trainer: 'Yes, anything else.'

Trainee: 'Well, all that nervous laughter.'

Trainer: 'Good . . . anything else.'

(Note: The 'good' here is a positive encouragement which gives the trainee a little more confidence to go on.)

Trainee: 'Well, when she was talking she seemed to be twitching around her mouth and her eyes were watery.'

(Note: The cue of the eyes was not noted by the trainer.)

Trainer: 'Very good.'

Trainee: 'But I don't see how you managed to work out that she had all those problems from just that.'

Trainer: 'I didn't know before. But I had to offer her the opportunity to speak which meant . . .'

Trainee: 'You had to listen.'

In our judgement this is an excellent piece of teaching and required only $1\frac{1}{2}$ minutes between patients. The possible benefits to the trainee are unlikely to be achieved in many hours of lecturing.

If we can accept that the above consultation goes a long way to reaching the root of a patient's real problems, how may one get such a message across in the learning situation? It is not sufficient to say to a trainee, 'A patient may well come to you with some physical disorder that you can recognise. He may also come to you with a problem which is rooted in his family, or his place of work, or deep in his own personality. Thus you must be on the *qui vive* for these.' There would also be little effective learning if one simply played a tape of the consultation reproduced above and said, 'Go thou and do likewise.' All one would have done in either event would have been to have told the trainee that some of the suspicions he already had about general practice were true and to have shown him how a highly competent and perhaps unusual general practitioner handled the situation. A possible outcome of such 'teaching' might be that the trainee would opt for something 'safe' like pathology, and abandon general practice altogether.

We have to discover a teaching method which will allow the trainee to find his feet in a situation for which he is as yet untrained. Neither are so many of us general practitioner teachers trained to cope with such situations. If we can cope, it is because for most of us this capacity is empirical and derived from our experience.

One of the more optimistic beliefs about discovery learning is that the learner not only learns what he is expected to learn but he also, in passing, learns the method. Simply put, this means that if we chose to teach a student about democracy using authoritarian teaching methods, the student will learn and be able to regurgitate all the data we have fed him on democracy, but also he will learn the authoritarian behaviour patterns he has experienced from his teachers.

The trainer faces the difficulty of reconciling the 'manifest content' and the 'latent content' of a learning situation. The 'manifest content' is that which the teacher desires to teach, i.e. his educational objectives. The 'latent content' is whatever learning bonus which may be achieved *en route* to fulfilling the 'manifest content'. All learning situations have manifest and latent content.

The skills required to manage the patient whose consultation was related above might have been under normal circumstances acquired by the trainee only after several years in practice. Conventionally it is believed that the trainee is unable to learn such skills (or alternatively that the trainer is unable to teach them) during a period of training. The usual platitude voiced as an escape from a discussion of such matters is that the trainee is 'being introduced to a group of general principles which will help him to react to each situation as he finds it'. In the light of the last twenty years of educational research and experience it appears that this statement is as valid as an older escape clause concerning the production of army officers from distinguished playing fields.

As we shall hope to show in the next chapter on 'non-directive counselling' there are teaching techniques open to the trainer for use with his trainee in the pursuit of educational objectives, which can have real value in the surgery. All that needs to be recognised by the trainer is that he is capable of teaching a 'method' at the same time as he is teaching 'content'.

The 'content' of the consultation related may be identified as:

1. Clinical knowledge of the menopause
2. A high level of patient empathy
3. A capacity for recognising non-verbal cues
4. An ability to ask reflective questions
5. An ability to listen
6. The strength of character to recognise that personal solutions to another's problems, objective but personal appraisals of situations, and the habit of 'getting rid' of such patients as soon as possible with a solid dose of tranquillisers are not the best ways of teaching on this sort of problem.

The only objective in the above list of content which can be achieved by 'telling'-type teaching is the first. In order to ensure that the trainee learns something about the other five, the trainer must prise himself away from his traditionally acquired teaching methods and start to examine quite different approaches.

Chapter 10

SIMULATED EXPERIENCE

If we refer back to the model of the training process (q.v.) it can be seen that for some time the trainee will be kept at a distance from the reality of the professional situation for which he is being trained. The rationale for this derives from pragmatists in the field of training who have found that when attempting to develop new behaviours in a trainee it is likely that these will be more readily accepted and integrated by him if their early development takes place in an environment which is free from risk.

There are a series of distinct and sequential processes derived from experience which are helpful when one is attempting to teach behaviours. Learners seem to learn more effectively when these sequences are built into a training programme. The stages are as follows:

1. Exposure
2. Play
3. Familiarisation
4. Confrontation
5. Analysis and questioning
6. Acceptance (or rejection).

It may not be obvious but it is difficult to learn a new behaviour unless one has been informed of what it is one is expected to learn. Thus an essential part of the trainer's function is to define the broad outlines of what is expected of the trainee. The degree to which he should specify the exactitude of what is expected to be learned is a matter for debate, and depends to a great extent on the trainer/trainee relationship in its widest aspects.

It can be demonstrated in various ways that under defined circumstances the optimum results from learning situations may be best obtained by the effective matching of individuals demonstrating certain types of behaviour patterns.

Bass, in his book *Organisational Psychology* (1965), suggests that the behaviour of a 'boss' can be viewed along a scale from authoritarian into consultative (with a somewhat schizoid area in between). Subordinate behaviour can be seen ranging from 'totally committed' at one end of a similar to totally uncommitted at the other. 'Committed' and 'uncommitted' refer to the attitudes of the 'boss' and the subordinate to their organisation and to their jobs. A series of European Research Group on Management 'business games' has been constructed upon Bass' work.

When work situations are explored in a controlled setting, using these scales for each, certain postulates have been sustained. For example, highly committed subordinates prefer to work with consultative bosses, but authoritarian bosses prefer working with less committed subordinates. Uncommitted subordinates do not like the commitment-seeking behaviours of consultative bosses, preferring to have the responsibility for making decisions moved away from themselves.

Such propositions, found to occur at significant levels in our culture, have lessons for any trainer who is working in a hierarchial situation. The E.R.G.O.M. series of exercises are based upon the premise that intelligent people will 'discover' these relationships if the training environment is properly managed. It is arranged that the learners know only that the styles of behaviour referred to above are postulated and that they, the learners, are going to find out what happens when matches are arranged between varying behaviour styles of boss and subordinate. These exercises seek to allow learners to 'feel' what happens in these situations rather than to have them force-fed with theory.

These propositions, however, are not unique in their relevance to business management training. They help to illuminate the attachment situation. For example, it is possible to produce a series of case-studies (q.v.) indicating what happens in a doctor/patient situation when one of the behaviour styles referred to meets another, identifying in each case-study the implications for the trainee. It is also possible to write case-studies in which extremes of behaviour match or mismatch are indicated. Unfortunately the latter approach would require each situation to be spelled out in such detail that the learner would have to be programmed in such a way that he could recognise an ideal match or a specific mismatch, when all the possible variables came true. Programming to this extreme and depth could only be based upon the premises that interpersonal behaviours are rational and that all possible variables can be covered—assumptions which have no rational basis.

In the present state of our knowledge of the teaching/learning of behaviours there is no prescriptive way in which we can actually direct perfect behavioural responses to all situations. All we may do is to get a learner to the point at which he can be aware of different situations and aware of his own potential range of behaviours. It is therefore of little value to attempt to teach on such a primary basis as 'if you find a client who is apparently committed to seeking successful outcomes of interactions, then you must adopt a consultative behaviour pattern—but if you find a totally demotivated client then you must become authoritarian.'

It is a fact that we are not yet competent to turn highly authoritarian learners into highly consultative trainees. We might still expect in the first instance to bring such a learner to the point that he may recognise that his behaviour pattern is highly authoritarian, and that under certain circumstances this pattern of behaviour will not be adequate. If he can be brought to this realisation then it is possible that he *may* decide to explore ways in which he can add to his range of behaviours.

With these considerations in mind we continue our examination of certain teaching techniques which appear to have the potential to bring trainees face to face with those problems which stem from their own behaviour. The utility of the 'case-study' and 'role-playing' is that they are devices which enable trainers to require a trainee to place himself in a given situation and then to examine his own responses to that situation. What is more useful is that the real patient/client of whatever system is being studied is removed from the situation and thus is in no danger of harm. These methods of learning/teaching represent ways of commencing to fulfil 'exposure', 'play' and 'familiarisation', the stages 1, 2 and 3 outlined above.

The trainer and the trainee each will have roles ascribed to them in the context of their interactions, but the trainer must retain the role of teacher—continually feeding back to the learner/trainee that which he, the trainer, sees in the trainee's behaviour pattern.

There are various types of case-study each proclaimed by its protagonists as being the answer to all training problems. The commonest is that which outlines an incident—'a case'—and then proceeds to tell the trainee what a particular individual, not infrequently the trainer, did in those circumstances. The implication of this type of teaching is that the trainee would be expected to do likewise.

One example is *The Doctor–Patient Relationship* by Browne and Freeling (1968), where the authors report on a variety of cases. On the whole they permit of wide analysis by the reader and at times admit to error. The reader, however, could be left with the feeling that a series of prescriptions has been provided.

The weakness of this sort of case-study is that it can lead to laziness upon the part of the trainer if he treats examples as perfect prescriptions for all settings. Some years ago one of the authors experienced a not unusual outcome of this type of case-study when he presented one based on an actual situation which had occurred in a factory in the north of England. There was basically a problem of discipline, badly handled by a supervisor, with the consequence of a wholly unnecessary strike.

This case was presented in another factory not two miles away from the original one, as part of a programme designed to teach line managers something about personnel management policies. The actual conclusion of the strike had been achieved by an able personnel manager. He had used methods within the normal competence of a reasonable line manager who should have been expected to prevent the problem becoming a strike issue. The group of managers studying the case came to the conclusion that such a sequence of events could never occur in their factory because 'their own supervisors wore white coats rather than green overalls'. Six weeks later an identical sequence of events produced in their own factory an almost identical outcome to that which had been presented.

Simulation or 'gaming' is based upon theoretical concepts and considerable empirical research. Many of the great names of twentieth-century educational practice have at some stage in their career spent much of their time investigating the role of 'games' in learning patterns. It is not unusual to find games and simulations built into the education of the school child. The seminal John Dewey and Jean Piaget came to favourable conclusions about the utility of games and simulation. In attachment, however, we are dealing not with school children but with trainees in late adolescence and early adulthood.

Possibly the most relevant studies, relevant to the training situation, are those made by Moreno (1934) of adolescent girls living in the closed world of a reform institution. Moreno concluded that their confined atmosphere made it difficult for these girls to develop the necessary environmental responses for comfortable survival in the outside world. He conducted a long series of experiments in which he sought, by simulating social functions and roles, to enable them to formulate behaviour patterns helpful in the outside world. (For a good overview of Moreno's work see Gage, 1963.)

He came to the conclusion that his forms of role-playing had some positive advantages over real life experience simply because they enabled subjects to examine and test alternate courses of action in situations where they were free from the possible penalty of paying the price of error. The opportunity to do this was—and is—one major distinction between the training situation and full professional life.

These theoretical and research considerations lead us now to examine ways in which the techniques to be discussed may be most profitably used.

Our concern is so to construct learning situations for the trainee that he may be allowed to examine his own reactions and behaviours in a variety of situations.

The cases we describe are largely concerned with the outcomes of behavioural interactions. It will be seen that a wide variety of behavioural responses is possible. It is not so much, in any possible variation, a matter of 'right' or 'wrong' solutions as the opportunity to examine and analyse that is important.

The desired result is usually optimal because there are so many variables in each situation. What is important is that the trainee is enabled to achieve for himself, by analysis of each situation, that solution or solutions, which represent the optimum for that patient and that trainee at that point in time.

'Hindsight' is a stern professional affliction. In this context we mean that if information, sought but not elicited or available at the time, later proves that decisions then made were wrong or disadvantageous, one should pause before feeling guilty. In real life, however diligently one may seek, information of crucial importance to the doctor's decision and hence to patient care, may be either unavailable or not forthcoming. In the first instance one can hardly be conceived as culpable. In the second it may be that the more experienced, the better trained, or the more diligent might well have acquired this information. As a trainee, lacking in experience, undergoing the training process, it is perhaps more important to avoid making twice an initial guiltless mistake. *Experientia docet* only if one is receptive to learning. A mistake is not guiltless when repeated after an initial recognition and analysis.

The most common form of 'case-study' is a simple 'presentation' of a doctor/patient situation which concludes with the question, 'What does the doctor do now?'

Let us examine the possibilities in the form of an actual teaching situation.

Example I

Trainer: 'Your patient is a single girl aged 16 who comes to see you in your surgery and asks you to "put her on the pill". What do you do?'

From a wide variety of possible responses from the trainee let us consider four.

Trainee:
1. 'I would give her a prescription for the pill.'
2. 'I would not give her a prescription for the pill.'
3. 'Subject to my discovering no clinical contra-indications I would give her a prescription.'
4. 'I would ask her, "Do you want to talk about it, or have you made your mind up?".'

The trainer would have to ensure that, whatever the behaviour indicated by these responses, the clinical criteria for the provision of the pill were met. He might well therefore challenge response 1 and approve response 3 on clinical grounds. Apart from this factor responses 1 and 3 represent the opposite to response 2. Each of these responses indicates a behavioural stand by the trainee which may indeed be explored in depth, but no one of them indicates a concern for the behaviour of the patient.

Response 4, on the other hand, an 'open-ended' question, indicates the trainee's interest in exploring the patient's behaviour at the same time casting some light upon his own.

Each response provides the trainer with an opening to wide fields of exploration of the behaviour of the trainee in ways which can demonstrate to the latter his own motivations, beliefs and possibly prejudices.

What if the trainer has honestly held beliefs, on perhaps moral or religious grounds, which propel him to reject responses 1 and 3 out of hand? He must be prepared for the fact that a very perceptive trainee may well, unconsciously, 'counsel' (q.v.) him, leading him to display the components of his own behaviour pattern to himself! Certainly such a trainer will find 'counselling' a difficult technique to acquire for himself, at least in any type of problem where the trainee produces solutions, however ethical, which challenge his, the trainer's, firmly held opinions. For he must, when he presents a case to the trainee, be clear on what his learning objectives are. In this latter instance does he wish the trainee to 'learn' or rather to acquire his opinions? Would the trainer who supported response 3 then wish to encourage the development of the situation created by response 4? Would the trainer—privately supporting response 2—be prepared to continue the situation he could create by suggesting response 4 and letting the trainee commence to clarify and develop his own behaviours? Perhaps he should.

In order to manage this sort of situation the trainee needs to have time to examine the case and to formulate his response. Although no research is available to validate the claim, there appears to be some value in presenting a series of case-studies of this type allowing the trainee less and less time for the formulation of his responses. The theory behind this is simple, in that the doctor in a real-life doctor/patient relationship has comparatively little time to formulate his responses to the patient. It is valuable to attempt to approach as near to the constraints of the real situation as training will allow.

A second variation is the continuous case which is presented as a series of developing situations. An initial presentation is made and the trainee is required to respond to it. The trainee is then presented with a series of developments of the case each requiring a fresh response. Such cases can be built up from real-life situations and so, if properly constructed, in addition to displaying the trainee's own response, offer him useful insights into the workings of professional life. There appears to be one major drawback to the use of this technique and that occurs when the response in the real-life case was totally unlike the trainee's response in the study. The trainee may then reasonably claim that his training is becoming unrealistic in that he would not have permitted himself to get into such a mess!

Example II

The clinical situation simply displayed in example I could become the commencement of an extended case-study taken from the real-life experience of the trainer.

The same presentation of the problem is made and after it has been discussed the first development appears.

'After exploring her situation with her it was decided to give the patient a prescription for the pill. There were no clinical contra-indications and she appeared quite determined to sleep with her "steady boyfriend". She was well for six months and then came to see you again for another prescription. She complained of feeling depressed.'

QUESTION 1

Suggest three possible factors in the aetiology of her depression. Among many possible answers the trainer might expect to hear:

SAMPLE ANSWERS

A. A side effect of the pill.
B. An endogenous depression.
C. She has not been taking the pill regularly and is now pregnant. Her boy friend has disappeared. Parental discovery and disapproval, etc.

Discussion can follow on A. What evidence is there that this condition exists? Is it common? How may it be avoided or combatted? Are all preparations equally guilty (or not)? It is again important that organic problems are defined and then dealt with.

QUESTION 2

What do you do now?

SAMPLE ANSWERS

A. Prescribe antidepressants.
B. Prescribe amitryptiline at a dosage of whatever.
C. Stop the pill.
D. Ask her to tell me more about it.

The nicety of definition in response B should not obscure the fact that both it and responses A and C represent an 'opting out' on the part of the doctor, who is not, as his behaviour suggests, intending to probe further. Response D, or any response indicating the trainee's intention to continue to explore the patient's problem should be the type of response desired. The trainer may have to spend some time in order to achieve this type of response from the trainee. Indeed some trainers might be wiser if they were to explore their own behaviour expressed in their preferred answers.

The situation can then develop (as it did in real life) through depression reactive to parental disapproval and the 'cooling off' of her relationship with her satiated boy friend, to an attack of gonorrhoea acquired from a casual relationship, to her sudden death from pulmonary embolism a year later.

Certainly in this case the trainer is not presenting an ideal solution, but at each successive stage the trainee is made to clarify his reasons for decisions made and to predict their effects. The tragic ending to this patient's problems affords the opportunity to open the dark area of professional responsibility and of guilt, real or conceived, the consciousness that each practising clinician will one day meet reproachful ghosts, and how may one adapt to such heavy heavenly prospects.

The trainee has here been introduced to some of the less frequently discussed areas of professional responsibility in an intellectual fashion removed from the region of that reality which he must shortly face.

This type of sequentially expanded study is used in the examination for the M.R.C.G.P. A paper giving a fuller description of the method is available. One tends to forget that the methods used for learning/teaching also apply to 'examination', 'review' or assessment. The model of Professor Morris (q.v.) should be referred to again. Any learning content which is 'concrete' can be taught, and its retention and use may be assessed by 'concrete' methods. Those matters of learning content which we suggested might best be learnt by participation in contrived or real life 'learning situations' may best be examined or assessed by the observation of overt behaviour. The latter means, in the case of the trainee, 'on the job' assessment.

We discuss evaluation and assessment in a later chapter.

A third variation of the case-study is the 'incident analysis', a development attributed to Professor Piggors of the Massachusetts

Institute of Technology. In this technique the trainer has to prepare considerable quantities of material in advance. It involves the presentation of situations in which a considerable variety and number of factors are involved. The trainee is presented with only a skeletal introduction but from that point on he may ask questions of his trainer to elicit further information. He is only given the information which the trainer feels the trainee's questions merit. On the basis of the information gathered the trainee is expected to make decision(s). This approach to case-study has considerable numbers of devotees in the U.S.A. but its usage in the U.K. seems to be limited.

When we have used this technique students have frequently commented that it is the most interesting and absorbing form of case-study. From a teacher's point of view, however, there is almost undue effort required to produce only one study. It has proved more useful to rely upon real-life experience of patients, rather than to attempt to produce fictional studies. One such study used by the authors covers 18 sheets of closely-typed foolscap in great detail, plus a further 8 sheets concerned with general information.

At best, case-studies are limited as teaching tools. At a factual level all one can hope to teach is general principles. At greater depth one may be able to reflect to the trainee something of his own prejudices and assumptions but the 'case-study' technique is of even more limited value if used in isolation as a teaching/learning method.

The introduction of 'role-playing' into a situation adds a further dimension to the possible teaching value. 'Role-playing' is a technique unfamiliar to most trainees. The term smacks of R.A.D.A. or Marlon Brando. In fact it does not require so much 'acting' in a physical sense, it requires the feeling for the part of the patient. The conviction with which a 50-year-old balding male presents an illegitimately pregnant girl of 18 must perforce be limited. Yet the 50-year-old male trainer may well have several such girls as patients. He himself learns a great deal about them by thinking himself into such a role. The training process provides learning situations for the trainer as well as for the trainee. Role-playing makes each reflect more with care on what it means to be a doctor and, above all, a patient. It was Chekov, himself a doctor, who said that he would spend a substantial portion of time in their training to make medical students realise what it was like to be a patient.

Neither is it necessary nor desirable that the trainee should always play the doctor. His own insights will be deepened, his perceptions sharpened if he on occasions plays the patient. The fundamental purpose of training is to seek the earlier provision of better patient/client care. While it is essential that the trainee is helped towards self-understanding, he must, *pari passu*, be assisted to patient/client under standing. A role-play may arise out of any case-type situation as mentioned above. At Manchester one role-play has proved salutary, yet it simply requires a doctor to consult with a patient. The consultation takes place at different levels.

Example III

In this role-play the trainee has usually been required to play the part of the doctor. He is given the following information.

The patient:
Mr P. J., age 45. Married, 3 children (21M, 18F, 6M).
Qualifications M.Eng. A.M.I.Mech.E. He is an executive in an engineering business. Salary £5000 p.a.

He comes to see you in your surgery.

He complains of:
1. Abdominal pain.
2. Feeling tired.

P.H. Tonsillectomy aet 9.
Appendectomy aet 19.
tib. aet 22 (no sequelae).
Nil else except occasional U.R.Is.
F.H. Nil relevant.
You have not seen this patient or his family before.
They have only recently come on to your 'list'.

The person playing the patient, and we have each ourselves played this part and have used a professional actor, is given the brief shown below. He is also given plenty of time to study the facts, and to 'think' himself into the part.

Certain factual information must be asked for by the 'doctor' relating to the results of physical examination or investigations. This information is provided by the 'patient' (or preferably another person appropriately briefed). The 'doctor', perhaps the trainee, may thus wish to know the patient's haemoglobin figure. He will ask for this and be given the answer—either 'normal for the patient's age and sex', or the abnormal figure, whichever is appropriate. This applies to all requests for information which must be specific. Thus, 'I will now examine the patient's abdomen. What do I find?' will receive only a bland silent smile. The specific, 'I would now examine the abdomen to see if there were any localised tenderness, or enlargement of the liver or spleen,' would then produce the requested information. The person playing the 'doctor', usually the trainee, is fully briefed to this effect.

The brief for the 'patient' includes that displayed above and continues:

H.P.C. (to be elicited by the 'doctor').

PHYSICAL

For the past five months he has had epigastric pain of a burning nature, unrelated to meals but occurring both day and night. In the daytime pain can be produced by stooping; at night he feels the discomfort when he lies down and sometimes a 'burning' passes upwards to his mouth, with occasionally an acid eructation. He finds bicarbonate and 'Rennies' helpful.

He has not lost weight but does feel tired and feels he is getting short-tempered.

He is a teetotaller and does not smoke.

On examination he appears normal in weight for his height and age. He appears tense. When he shakes hands his hands are sweaty and warm.

This information will obviously only be elicited if asked for by the 'doctor'.

PHYSICAL EXAMINATION

Pulse	96 regular B.P. 140/90. C.V.S. otherwise normal.
C.V.S.	Slight tremor of hands only when arms extended palms down. K.Js brisk, but equal. All other functions normal.
Abdomen	N.A.D.
R.S.	N.A.D.

Nil else abnormal.

INVESTIGATIONS

1. Blood. Hb 9·5 g. Nil else abnormal.
2. Stools. Occult blood present in modest quantities on three separate occasions.
3. Barium. swallow and meal. Sliding hiatus hernia. No indication of malignancy.

Nil else abnormal.

DIAGNOSIS

Hiatus hernia.

TREATMENT

1. Avoid stooping, bed sloped up from foot.
2. Dry meals—fluids in between.
3. Alkalies +/− phenobarb.

PSYCHOLOGICAL AND SOCIAL (to be elicited by the 'doctor')

He has had for some months increasing feelings of anxiety, including early waking even after the initial physical discomfort has been relieved, not accompanied by return of discomfort. He has twice been passed over for promotion and feels that at 45 he has reached his peak in his present or any other firm.

He might come to terms with this but his wife's ambitions are difficult to thwart. She has not supported him but nagged. Relationships are strained and he fears—but has no proof—that she may be entering into a liaison with a mutual and more successful 'friend' recently widowed.

The eldest child—a son—has been sent down from university, is on drugs and shacked up with a fellow sufferer. The wife blames the patient for this.

His short temper has led to further problems at work to a degree that he believes his job to be in jeopardy. He will relate this to son, wife and/or job.

He will admit to cancerphobia but will be prepared to accept reassurance on this point—if it is offered on the evidence of history, examination and investigation.

This patient's record, drawn up from real life, offers wide opportunities for the trainee. He is presented with a straightfoward pathogomonic history, readily confirmed by radiology. But there is here no 'life-threatening' situation. The patient will be found to be relieved of his abdominal pain by the simple measures normally proposed for the management of hiatus hernia.

There are clues—the early waking even when the pain has been relieved for example—that the patient has more than a simple physical problem. The 'doctor' has to identify the psychosocial problems as well and then propose solutions. How does he do this? How will he tell, advise or counsel his patient? Will he wish to 'see' the wife and son?

All these and many more questions are to be discussed and explored. The original real-life happenings are irrelevant. What is relevant is the heightening of the trainee's awareness of whole person medicine and an opportunity for him to practise and develop his burgeoning skills in a risk-free situation.

In the case presented the real-life ending was the patient's suicide. Again this cannot be regarded as a prescriptive perfect solution. But which trainer has not had such a sad experience? Which trainee is not, in his future professional life, going to face similar problems? Whether the real-life doctor might have achieved a happier solution or not is immaterial. Neither can it be certain that such a role-playing experience may of itself prevent the trainee from experiencing a like result. What is relevant is that a series of such role-playing studies, each adequately analysed, helps the trainee to prepare for real-life experience and makes clearer to him the difficulties and possibilities of his future involvement with patients in 'risk-full' situations. It adds to his experience on which much of his future decisions and behaviours will depend.

This sort of case/role approach can be invaluable as a tool for making students realise that the general practitioner, even when he has made a correct physical diagnosis and has prescribed, is still left with a complex of problems at the family, psychological and social levels with which he should attempt to deal.

This is a point at which training can become very difficult indeed. There is in the practice of medicine no clear definition of a cut-off point in the doctor/patient relationship, and this applies in particular to general practice. Some general practitioners assert that their responsibility has ended when they have diagnosed and prescribed. Others take a broader view of the social system within which they operate. They then choose to enquire, with the intention of treating them, into psychological and social problems. We have no doubt as to which view is preferable if the best of medical care is desired. Those general practitioners, however, who believe in a multifactorial concept of illness must face up to the complexities of the task of developing in the trainee the necessary values which will enable him to develop with the same concept in mind.

To provide medical care at the level of the whole person in a family in an environment presents a general practitioner with a variety of problems. He may feel that he need not, himself, face them. To do so he will require in addition to medical skills, social skills and skills of interpersonal relationships. There is evidence that role-playing may help to develop such skills. Role-playing and case-study, however, must not be seen as a substitute for reality. They are only intended to be an introduction to reality. If they are seen as techniques which have some value in the development of skills for the trainee they are then in proper perspective. It must be realised that the unconsidered usage of these techniques may only produce trainees who are good actors rather than real doctors who will give real care to real people.

Chapter 11

COUNSELLING AND THE REFLECTIVE TECHNIQUE

Developing the theme of our comments upon non-directive teaching we turn now to the nature and purpose of non-directive counselling. There are essentially seven governing principles in the organisation of this activity as an educational process in training.

1. Enable the trainee to define his own problem(s).
2. Enable the trainee to generate his own solution(s) to his own problem(s).
3. Enable him to examine the implications of his own solution(s).
4. Enable him to select his own course(s) of action.
5. Never be guilty of offering to the trainee problems which he does not produce for himself.
6. Never be guilty of offering to the trainee solutions to his own problems.

Or most important of all:

7. Never assist him with the working out of his own solutions.

Several participants and observers of the Manchester training programmes have commented upon an apparent similarity between this process and some forms of psychotherapy. It would appear, however, that there is one quite significant difference between psychotherapy and counselling. Psychotherapy often involves substantial transference between therapist and client. Indeed one must add that transference is an essential tool of psychotherapeutic practice. Little, if any, transference is noticeable in a pure counselling process. (For a clear and readable definition of the concept of transference see Dewald, 1964.) There is the further point that the decision to use counselling is also dependent upon a prejudgement by the counsellor that the client is capable of coping with the counselling process. In all senses of the word then the client is adjudged 'normal'. Thus, if one is dealing with a situation in which the client patently cannot cope then counselling is an inappropriate technique. (Dr Gareth Lloyd has coined a word which is useful in this context 'acopia'—the inability to cope—his view is that this can be a recognisable condition.)

The technique, fundamental to this type of counselling, is that of the reflected question. Very rarely does the counsellor ever answer directly a question put to him by the client. He takes each question posed to him and turns it round into a question for the client to try and answer. If the client fails to respond to the question then the counsellor rephrases the same question until he receives an answer. Once the counsellor has provided an answer to a question he has commenced the process of becoming a prop upon which the client will lean. Transference may also start to appear in a question and answer situation, unless due care is taken by the counsellor.

Here is a series of examples of reflected questions:

Patient: 'Do you think all this is caused by the change of life?'
Doctor: 'What does the change of life mean to you?'
Patient: 'Do you think I ought to discuss this with my wife?'
Doctor: 'How do you feel about discussing it with your wife?'
Patient: 'I feel I ought to go into a different line of work, don't you?'
Doctor: 'Have you thought about what a different line of work will mean to you?'

When analysing the interaction which takes place in a counselling situation it is possible to discern three roles. The essence of the interaction is contained in the two roles of 'help giving' and 'help receiving'. These roles, however, are not identified with counsellor and counsellee. In any 'help giving' process the 'help giver' must initially be given help in order to be able to help. Even in a straightforward 'clinical' situation, during a physical examination the doctor would be quite at a loss if the patient refused to co-operate by submitting to examination. History-taking is impossible if the patient will not respond to questioning.

The way in which we may determine who is the counsellor and who is the counsellee is by the observation of two factors, 'Who is asking reflected questions?' and 'Who is controlling the flow and direction of the process?' This last is the most difficult question to explain in words. Possibly the simplest way is to ask the reader to recall consultations in which it has suddenly occurred to him that the conversation he thinks he is having with the patient is not the same as the conversation which the patient thinks he is having with the doctor. In order to achieve this realisation it is necessary to be able to observe the conversation almost from outside it.

Having made such a discovery the doctor might then seek to change the way in which the conversation is going. To do this requires a piece of 'process observation' in which the counsellor is not only listening to the words used in the conversation but is also keeping a check on its direction, its flow and its dynamics. He is continually reviewing the conversation against such criteria as, 'Are we talking "to" each other or talking "at" each other?' 'Are we getting anywhere with this line of thought?' 'Do I need a new strategy at this point?'

The third role then to be adopted by the counsellor is that of 'process observer'. Thus there are in effect two persons and three parties involved in counselling.

The counsellor has two functions. He has to act as a counsellor, but at the same time he also has to act as an observer of the process he is involved in. We have not found it difficult to present these ideas to general practitioners because so many of them have on occasions been aware of evaluating the 'process' of even a straightforward physical examination. Our experiences with trainees although more limited, have shown us that they too are receptive of these ideas and as quick to perceive their additional application to patient care as have been their trainers.

The reader may be concerned to discover how he may learn this technique. Counselling is one of those activities which can only be 'learned by doing'. It is not possible in the format of a book to enable the learner to undergo that essential experiential learning which only well-constructed behavioural programmes can achieve. What can be attempted is a presentation of counsellee/trainee-type questions, which the reader has to seek to reflect. The reader is invited to study the following questions and to attempt to rephrase them in such a way that the questioner would be required to answer them for himself.

Trainee: 1. 'Well, doctor, how do you think I am getting on with my training programme?'
Trainee: 2. 'I think I managed that patient rather well, don't you?'
Trainee: 3. 'How should I approach this patient?'
Trainee: 4. (The seductive approach.) 'I thought you handled that situation rather well. How did you do it?'

(Some suggested answers to these questions are at the end of the chapter on page 97.)

We have found that the most effective device to facilitate the learning of counselling has been to take two individuals who wish to learn of it and to get them to provide each other with a *real* problem from their own work situation. The counsellee tells the counsellor what he thinks his problem is. The counsellor then has to ask questions of the counsellee until he reaches the point where he too feels that he understands what the problem really is. For the inexperienced in this situation it is always worth testing the hypothesis that when the counsellor comes to the conclusion that he understands the counsellee's problem, he also comes to the conclusion that he should try to delve a little deeper. After three such essays he usually discovers that his initial understanding was imperfect.

This training technique may well fail, however, if an individual poses a problem which he invented for the occasion.

It is essential to ensure that at no time does the counsellor actually provide direct answers to the questions posed by the counsellee. Also at no time does he attempt to provide any answers or opinion on the counsellee's self-defined problem.

We have found this to be the most difficult learning task for general practitioners because so much of their training and experience has led them to offer (and their patients to expect) firm opinions on and solutions to most of the problems with which their patients present to them. The training activity, therefore, has to concentrate upon the exhibition of an old behaviour—that of listening—with learning the new behavioural change of *not* offering interpretation and advice.

The further problem of learning the sequences of the technique has not, to date, appeared to be a major one, in so far as it follows a normal and straightforward decision-making routine. One does not begin to look at answers to problems until one knows which problems one faces. In the counselling situation, having defined the problem(s), the optimal course of action is to generate as many alternative solutions as possible, rather than to permit the acceptance of the solution first proposed. Before finally guiding the selection of a specific solution it is worth the trouble of analysing the likely effects were one to permit its adoption.

Underlying the counselling activity are a number of important general propositions. The first of these concerns the nature of collective decision-making. There is now considerable acknowledgement of the fact that those who are obliged to turn decisions into action are more likely to be committed to that action if they feel they have been party to the decision(s) which determined it. If they are implementing decisions made by others then their commitment is less reliable.

This observation on human behaviour is also related to beliefs about the need for self-determination in life. If, for example, it is important that individuals learn new 'coping' behaviours, then it is better that they learn the full meaning of these behaviours for themselves, rather than, in a situation which is essentially temporary, relying upon some outside person or agency for support.

Finally, in terms of learning, non-directive counselling can be used as an essential adjunct to the process of 'discovery' learning, of which one quality is that individuals not only learn what they are expected to learn, but that they also learn the method of learning. If we accept the Oslerian view of the professional need for life-long learning then there should be a permanent process of self-direction towards new learning goals. We might then be able to get away from the situation in which so many people conclude their full-time education in the belief that their learning is also completed. We agree with Charles Carter who said, 'Education is not an act of salvation after which one is safe for eternity.'

As to the question of when one applies this technique, it is not possible to frame general rules. It is possible to use it even when factual learning is concerned. For example, if a student demonstrates a marked lack of clinical knowledge in a particular area, one approach would be to instruct him, i.e. to 'tell' him. This, however, would presuppose that the learner's sole problem was a specific area of clinical factual deficiency. It is possible that his lack of information in this area is indicative of a much deeper problem, namely his inability (or worse, unwillingness) to seek out sources of information. Hence in response to his request for specific information a counselling-type reply could be, 'Do you know where to look for information which will enable you to answer that particular question?'

Should the answer come back in the form of 'no' the first impulse to retort 'Why not?' might be resisted in favour of finding out what he actually does know about sources of material.

Much depends upon the teacher's judgement of the trainee. It is said about discovery learning that people may spend weeks 'discovering' the wheel, so that should the trainee simply require a piece of factual knowledge there is usually no point in spending hours seeking it out. On the other hand, should it become apparent that the trainer is becoming a resource for every bit of information the trainee finds himself lacking, then the trainer is faced with the problem of somehow guiding the trainee towards examining his own approach to learning.

In the more problematic areas of learning, for example that learning which is necessary for dealing with people, one is faced with a galaxy of teaching/learning problems. It is simply not good enough to present one's own behaviour pattern as a model (or for that matter anyone else's) which the trainee is then expected to learn. This approach produces poor actors who have no feeling for the part they are playing. It is also unthinking behaviour on the part of the trainer. His own roles have been learned from a wide range of experience which he is quite unable to share with the trainee. It is almost like trying to explain the 'feeling' of toothache to someone who has never experienced that pain.

Non-directive counselling is a useful device to examine any learning which may have taken place, after learning activity has been experienced. For example, if a trainee has just 'managed' a case in the consulting room, the traditional teacher/trainer would simply provide a personal appraisal of that situation. The appraisal, however, would be most often based upon a view of how he, the trainer, would have handled the situation—which is only a partly valid approach. To provide a more valid appraisal the trainer must accept that the trainee has insights into the situation which he, the trainer, does not share.

The trainee may very well desire a full debriefing from the trainer, in the form of a 'If I were in your position I would have done this or that.' Whilst this is a most useful approach at a basic level, it has the inbuilt danger of becoming a model of finality.

A more effective way of debriefing an experience is to begin by turning the trainee back in upon himself by asking, 'How well do you feel you managed that situation?' This sort of approach is much more likely to produce an open-ended exploration of the situation than any other. The ideal outcome of such a situation is one in which the trainee feels completely free to highlight his own shortcomings and failures so that he may improve his performance in similar areas on subsequent occasions. This ideal, however, takes a long time to achieve and it may well be necessary to concentrate the trainee's attention on areas which, *prima facie*, he feels he has accomplished well.

The questioning form here is rather more specific. The phrasing of the question must delineate the specific area to which the trainer wishes to call attention, but, and this is significant, it ought not to contain any indication that the trainer has already passed a value judgement. Let us highlight this by an example. A trainee has just completed a consultation with a patient which he feels he has accomplished well. During this interview the trainer felt that at a certain point the trainee has already made up his mind and was no longer listening to the patient. During this phase the patient made a 'by the way doctor' offer which was considered important by the trainer but was apparently not noted by the trainee.

The trainer's objectives then are to discover whether or not:

1. The trainee did 'shut off' to the patient.
2. If he did was he aware of the possible significance of 'by the way' offer.

In this situation the trainer could simply say, 'I feel that you shut off to that patient three-quarters of the way through the consultation. During that time while you were making noises meant to indicate to her that you were listening, you demonstrated to me that you were not, because as she went out she said, "By the way, doctor, can I get haemorrhoid ointment on prescription?" As you had been examining her nose it seems unlikely that you gained any information about her other end. It is important that you are alert to the final remarks made by a patient, because if you read your "Browne and Freeling" you will discover that these remarks are sometimes of considerable importance.'

To this a good defence by the trainee would be, 'Yes, I did hear her question about the ointment and I replied "yes", therefore I answered her question.'

The trainer is now up against the wall because most of the next moves are already predicted.

'But do you not think that she might have been worried about something for her to raise that question with you at that point?'

'If she was so concerned surely she would have raised it during the consultation?'

And so it can go on and gradually assume the form of a nice 'if and but' academic debate.

A more effective approach might be a well-prepared strategic development of a sequence of questions.

'I think that interview went rather well, I would now like to concentrate your attention upon the last few minutes. How do you feel you handled them?'

'Can you recall what the patient's final words were?'

'Her final words were, "Doctor, can I get haemorrhoid ointment on prescription?" What sort of significance do you attach to these?'

'As some patients are leaving the consulting room, there is a tendency for them to say important things; have you ever noticed this habit in the past?'

'Why do you think that some patients are given to saying important things to the doctor, almost as they are leaving the room?'

'Assuming that some patients do this, what does that mean for the doctor?'

This could be a prepared sequence of questions which the trainer could use, although he might find that he does not need to use them all. On paper they look like Queen's Counsel leading a reluctant witness to say things he does not really want to say.

Unfortunately, print does not allow one to express the words as one would do in normal speech. The missing factor is best described by the term 'neutrality of tone', which neither can be said to threaten nor does it appear to condone. The important point to appreciate is that one is not leading the trainee to conclusions which are there already—but one is hoping that he will reach conclusions of his own accord. If, in the case above, the point were reached at which the trainee claimed that he did not care much for patients who said things as they left the room, no amount of influence will affect him as much as missing a few important 'by the ways' in a real-life situation. One of the problems with experiential learning is that one must have 'experiences' in order to appreciate the value and meaning of experience.

During a counselling session the most directive behaviours of the counsellor are demonstrated at those points in time when he decides to move the session forward from one phase to the next. Earlier we concerned ourselves with the problem of the trainee who, presenting a particular deficiency of knowledge, revealed a personal inability to use sources properly. This is a not uncommon situation for trainees in many disciplines and it can be due to a wide variety of causes. In some cases it may simply be that they are quite unaware of sources and thus need to learn of them. The more problematic cases are those of the trainees who know where the sources are but are unable or unwilling to use them.

If one has reached the stage where the trainee has admitted that he does know where the sources are, but for a variety of reasons does not use them, there is little point in driving him to the possible conclusion that he is lazy. The trainer may find himself very annoyed to discover that trainees are not as he believes himself to be. The urge to express his feelings must be resisted. A more useful approach would be to commence with such statements as the following, 'Fine, we are now at the point where you are saying to me that you recognise that you have several gaps in your pattern of knowledge; you know where the sources of material are; you are not at this point in time using these sources. Assuming that tomorrow you come up against another such deficiency—how do you think you ought to go about solving your problem?'

This is an easy situation to manage and has fairly obvious outcomes. In a more complex situation such as that presented by the 'listening but not hearing trainee' a transition would have to be made at the point at which the trainee has decided that final words may be important and that 'listening but not hearing' behaviour may well be a hindrance to the doctor's effectiveness. If the trainee accepts this he must then be moved onwards to examine how he will behave in future situations. A possible form of words might be, 'We have now reached the situation where you are saying to me that you think that 'by the ways' could be important, but you have also recognised that at some point in the development of a consultation you make up your mind and cease to listen to the patient. How do you think you are going to overcome this?'

A predictable outcome of this situation is that the counsellee in his next consultation will rush through its first part in order to get to the end where he will listen for his first recognisable 'by the way'. The counsellor requires a deal of patience.

The termination of a counselling session is also quite difficult, especially so because many people suffer from the delusion that once they have made a decision they have done all there is to do. The fact that decisions have to be turned into action is sometimes relegated to a 'be all right on the night' situation. The counsellor should be sure that the counsellee is certain that he knows what his final decision is, and has worked through its consequences. The counsellor should also be certain that the counsellee is aware, that when he leaves the counselling situation, he is going away to put his decision into action. Thus the third phase of counselling is almost as important as defining the problem. The counsellor must continually get the counsellee to reflect upon the consequences of his possible solutions. In this area there is some room for argument over the degree of control in which the trainer/counsellor should indulge. If one took a theoretical position to absurd lengths it could be accepted that if a trainee was convinced that going to the North Pole would help him in his lack of clinical knowledge then he must be allowed to try to get there. The counsellor should feel that the proposed solution of the counsellee is optimal in all the circumstances—even if only because it will quickly be discovered if it be ineffective. A unique feature of the caring professions is that there is so often a live third party to the training. In the case of general practice this is the patient. It matters little what the professional setting may be, if it requires the patient/client to be a third party to training, the patient/client must not be allowed to suffer or in any way be harmed because of the training process. It could be argued that a lack of training process might obviate harm for a patient here and now and simply shift the timing of any inadvertent harm by the untrained to the hereafter. But the trainee is in the here and now situation.

The trainer may on occasions be in a position to know that certain courses of proposed action by his trainee/counsellee may lead to some harm being done to the patient/client. He cannot allow this harm to be done, but his dilemma is that if he says so outright he will destroy the counselling relationship. A possible compromise in such a situation might well be the 'hypothetical outcome' question: 'If you decide on this course of action and you find that the outcomes are so and so, how do you think you will manage that situation?'

More directive forms of control lie in questions such as, 'Do you think that you have really generated enough possible solutions to this particular problem to give you a valid choice?' 'At this point in our activity we are concerned with providing you with as many alternatives as possible before you actually make your choice. Do you think that you have, at this point in time, as many alternatives as you think you are capable of generating?'

This sort of intervention, whilst it is completely alien to the philosophy of the activity may well be necessary simply to protect the patient/client. As with all other aspects of human behaviour self-determination contains an element of risk and luck. Whilst it is perfectly acceptable for an individual to learn by his own mistakes (indeed that may be a desirable learning situation) it is not acceptable for those mistakes to be perpetrated upon people—who are so often also 'the training material'.

This point may well be reinforced by examining the consequential behaviour into which counselling leads trainers. It has already been stated that the counsellor should never become involved with his counsellee's working out of their own solutions. Once the counsellee has made his decision the counsellor leaves him to get on with it. Even if the counsellee comes back and says that his solution did not work the most appropriate behaviour is to start all over again from the beginning. In the training situation we are discussing it is quite probable that the counsellor will find himself in the situation where he is watching the counsellee work out his solution for real. If he interferes in that working out he has nullified all the work achieved to date. His interference will be seen as two things by the counsellee:

1. A somewhat belated, but none the less overt criticism of himself.
2. An example of 'this is how you ought to have done it' training.

This sort of intervention then is to be avoided at all costs. It means, therefore, that before the trainee decides to implement a course of action involving patients, the trainer must be certain that this course of action will not adversely affect the patient.

(Essential follow-up reading for this reading is Shertzer and Stone, 1968, and Rogers, 1965.)

SUGGESTED ANSWERS TO QUESTIONS ON PAGE 90

Answer 1: 'Well let us begin by finding out what your own feelings about your progress are?'

Answer 2: Several possible routes here.
'What leads you to feel so well about that interaction?'
or
'How do you think the patient feels now?'

Answer 3: A difficult one to which the 'how do you think you should approach him' is not sufficient.
A more forcing approach might be:
'Do you have any anxieties about this particular patient?'
or
'Try putting yourself in his position and think out aloud what he might be expecting from you as he comes in.'

Answer 4: Before providing the answer to this question, if you allowed a little smirk, or glow of pride to cross your face you were raped rather than seduced, however much you enjoyed the experience. 'What elements did you observe which you feel contributed to any success which might have occurred?' It may hurt to say something so self-effacing, but now the seducer has been seduced and he does not know how you did it.

Chapter 12

PLAYING FOR REAL

So far we have looked at techniques which concern the teacher and the student in a 'telling' relationship and in a 'playing' relationship, i.e. in case-study and role-play.

The consultation is that part of general practice through which its major activity is discharged. The consultation is thus the chief learning situation for all trainees.

Case-study and role-play techniques have here a clear introductory value, and we would expect that any trainer who takes his task seriously will have at least considered the use of these techniques before letting the trainee have full responsibility for his patients.

We thus reach the point at which an all-important third party, the patient, is introduced into the transaction for there is a limit to the extent to which 'non-reality', in the ways which we have described, may be used. While the trainee has eventually to cope with the patient one of the purposes of attachment training is that he should first come face to face with his patient in a setting where the maximum amount of learning can be derived from the transaction. One function of a trainer is to maximise that learning. We may consider the possibility that the patient may also take part in the teaching/learning process, but for the moment we will concentrate upon the role of the trainer in the situation where he is the prime promoter of learning.

We have suggested that as soon as the two parties involved in the attachment come together they will discuss in some detail what the trainee wishes to achieve. If we accept the concept that a general practitioner cannot be effective unless he is competent at consultation, there can be no doubt that, even although the trainee may be unaware of this concept, the trainer must bring it to his attention.

The consultation must be approached in a systematic manner and the previously noted format for learning is again useful. At a low level of exposure one merely has the trainee 'sitting in' on surgeries to observe what happens. Although some trainers may wish to permit the trainee to indulge only in observation there must surely come a point at which the trainee is himself directly involved. There will undoubtedly be many occasions when the trainer has the advantage of information not immediately available to the trainee, certainly in the context of the patient, and/or his family's, pre-relationship with the trainer.

It seems logical therefore that, if the trainee is going to achieve the maximum of learning from a consultation, he must at least have had access to his trainer's notes and to any other information which the trainer may be able to give him before the consultation actually starts. A great constraint upon learning from the consultation is that surgery sessions are based upon time schedules which are often outside the trainer's control, and hence make it more difficult for teaching/learning to take place. The trainer is thus faced with a dilemma. What is his prime purpose? If it be only to practice medicine then the trainee must take second place. If it be to enable the trainee to learn about general practice then the patient must take second place. Whatever decision is based upon such a structure of alternatives then it must be made clear by the trainer to himself and to his trainee before the surgery/learning session begins.

It is usually necessary to seek a compromise between these two situations. Greater flexibility is possible if the trainer is prepared to reduce his normal patient consultation rate, if only by one or two per hour.

An ideal introductory phase would be a prepatient briefing of the trainee by the trainer, followed by the patient consultation, followed by a discussion between trainer and trainee on what happened.

The next stage is that in which the trainer decides to hand over part or all of some consultations to the trainee. If we follow our previous learning model (q.v.) then this is clearly a stage of play and/or familiarisation. It is not possible to remove wholly for the trainee the risks of the situation, but they will have been minimised if the trainer has made it clear that he will provide help if it seems to be required. Here again audiotape recordings can be a valuable asset to learning.

Even experienced general practitioners may be surprised when they first hear themselves performing on tape—as we have been. For those who doubt this a reading of the first chapter of *The Dynamics of Interviewing* (Kahn and Cannell, 1957) will indicate what may happen in a real-life situation.

While every consultation has an objective(s) and a strategy(ies), these are not normally taught in medical school. Under the more usual circumstances of a young doctor's development this approach to consultations has to be learned by trial and error. The advantage of studying consultations in the ways we suggest is that the trainee does not have to rely upon bad experiences for his feedback, he may simply get it from his trainer.

One goal of training is to accelerate learning and we return to our original thesis that an important purpose of attachment is to develop in the trainee the learning not so much of medicine but of the behaviour patterns through which he will practice medicine.

At a given point to be decided by the trainer and the trainee a patient will be handed over to the latter who will accept total responsibility for the whole process, without any interruption from his trainer. Clearly there are problems here which will have to be considered. It is unthinkable that the trainer will be prepared to allow a trainee to make a wrong or incomplete diagnosis, or worse to offer a wrong prescription even if his diagnosis is correct.

A development of this approach to the introductory phase might be to commence the debriefing with the question to the trainee, 'What would you have done in that situation?'

Should time prove to be too great a constraint an alternative device could be to record on audiotape all consultations and to use these tapes as the basic material of a teaching/learning session when time can be found. The advantage of the tape-recorded consultation is that there is a full replay rather than the simple recall of a situation which has passed. There is also the possibility of being selective so that consultations which have limited teaching potential can be ignored. Selection, of course, can be made by both trainer and trainee so that the trainee is also able to exercise some control over his learning situations. Tape recordings later discussed have the further advantage that debriefings can be fuller. Thus, if an important part of a consultation is a background family history this can be described in greater detail than might have been possible at the time of the actual consultation. The patient's permission to make audiotape recordings must always be obtained.

The importance of this stage of training is that the trainee can begin to direct his attention away from his discipline and focus it upon the appropriate behaviour patterns contained in any given situation. Unless a wrong clinical diagnosis has been made, the question, 'How do you think I handled that situation?' has got absolutely nothing to do with clinical, in the sense of 'organic', medicine.

The general practitioner trainer has certain traditional views about his patients and these views are firmly coloured in the U.K. by his ethical and statutory obligations to them. His 'nothing like leather' attitude is an expression of his belief that no one at all can care for his patients as well as he can. It is from this attitude, representing at best his dedication, that there stem his difficulties in accepting the concepts of team work and delegation. It is this attitude which tempers his decision-making as to when he will permit his trainee to have personal responsibility for patients, and the degree of responsibility which he will then allow.

At the same time the trainer will realise that the trainee must have such responsibility. His necessary decisions will be based upon his assessment of his trainee, an assessment supported by the reviews of their preceding interactions. These assessments will further assist the trainer to select those patients for whom his trainee should have responsibility, and also to plan his trainee's exposure to more difficult patients and problems. However much responsibility for patients is provided for the trainee, his trainer still has the duty of training added to his own inevitable responsibility for the patients seen by the trainee.

Fortunately the process of review can help the trainer to satisfy these twin duties. There is unlikely to be time to discuss fully each patient seen by the trainee and the outcomes of the several consultations, but various forms of sampling can be helpful. The trainer can select those patients to be discussed with the trainee. He can arrange perhaps that some patients are later seen by him and that future discussion with the trainee will then take place. The trainee should be encouraged to 'consult' with his trainer so that together they may on occasion see particular patients. The patient records of the trainee will be expected to meet with his trainer's approval for they must fit in with the accepted pattern of the practice. These records can be used to provide the information upon which the trainee may be required to defend his therapy and/or his patient management.

'Patient management' is a term which refers more to the way in which a doctor relates to his patients than to the way in which he diagnoses and prescribes.

Whichever methods are used, the trainer and trainee may each expect to receive feedback upon their performance from two other sources—the patients themselves and other members of the practice team.

Neither patients, nor receptionists, for example, are slow to talk, and their likes and dislikes become known quite quickly. Patients can, and do, 'vote with their feet', and in the training situation this can be traumatic for either or both the trainer and the trainee. The patient's vote is not often cast in the dramatic direction of leaving the practice, although that may occasionally happen. It is, however, not unusual that a trainer feels hurt or threatened because some of his patients 'vote' to see his trainee. The trainer must learn to rationalise this event. He may take comfort in the theory that it is a recognition of the good job which he is doing in training, but he will be wiser to accept that, firstly it is inevitable on occasion, and that secondly it is brought about by a variety of factors.

Two of these are important and obvious. The one that a fresh personality and a new look at his problems have been presented to the patient who thus may literally receive a 'second opinion'. This may even on occasion prove more correct or more acceptable to the patient. The other factor is that the trainee, by definition, should have available to him more time with his patients—at least when he is first presented with them. This means that he has more time to offer to his patients that faculty which they prize so highly—listening. Perhaps a not so obvious factor is that the peripatetic patient may well be attempting to manipulate both trainer and trainee. Comforting each other they may learn how they may manage the patient.

It was that unlikely doctor Falstaff who said, 'It is the disease of not listening, the malady of not marking that I am troubled withal.' Admittedly Falstaff made his comment to an innkeeper when discussing the sordid matter of debts, but his statement, so valuable in itself for all practising clinicians, can be construed as defining two major possible ills of the general practitioner, those of not listening to patients, and of not keeping good records. The time provided by the slower work tempo of the trainee should afford active protection against them.

On his part the trainee can regard these advantages as some compensation for the behaviour of those patients who, also inevitably, will direct their feet back to his trainer. The latter after all has the advantages of his own patient relationships earned by acknowledged service. The trainee may only accept this fact for it represents the situation which he will expect eventually to achieve for himself.

'Going solo' for the first time is always a great event in the career of a pilot. If his training up to that point has not been sound, if assessments have been mistaken, then it may indeed be his last. The doom of such finality does not hang over the trainee on his first 'solo' while every care must be taken to see that his patient is safe. Nevertheless it still represents an important stage in his professional development. It is a stage for which both he and his trainer instructor have prepared with care, one of which each will gratefully record the successful completion. It is the end of the beginning.

From this time on the trainee will require considerable assistance from his trainer. Crombie (1963) has reported on the guilt feelings born of inadequacy from which so many young doctors in general practice are bound to suffer. It is in this area in particular that the trainer's use of non-directive methods can be so helpful in the maintenance of the trainee's morale and the gradual build-up of not only his professional competence, but of his professional confidence. The trainer is ideally placed to drop words in season both to patients and colleagues which can smooth the trainee's path. The latter will still contain enough obstructions to challenge the trainee striving to make his own way through professional life.

The trainee will be wise to recognise that, in his exposure to an able man of perhaps strong personality and wide effectiveness as a doctor, there is a danger that his critical faculty can be obscured by admiration or even by affection. This is an area where the achievement of self-understanding is of great importance for both trainer and trainee. The trainer should not be a 'Nellie' who unconsciously transmits both his strengths and weaknesses. Recognising the latter he may seek to remedy them and keep an alert eye for their appearance in the trainee. The attachment situation contains much learning for both parties.

CHAPTER 13

EVALUATION AND ASSESSMENT

Every educational process needs evaluation. The teacher needs to know that his educational objectives have been met. The learner needs to know that he has achieved that which was expected of him. Both teacher and learner need to know how they have performed. Learning situations extending over many years at school, during training and in the practice of a profession provide together for the learner a life-long operational armamentarium of knowledge, skills and attitudes.

Yet there is ample evidence to show that the performance of a doctor, while depending to some degree on these broad three factors, is more specifically influenced by his social and interpersonal skills, his self-knowledge, the attitudes he displays, and various factors of personality and intellect. None of these parameters may be measured accurately in precise numerate terms and in general they must all be assessed by observation of overt behaviour when satisfactory grading should be possible. This is what is intended in the traditional clinical examination of various professional medical bodies.

The 'overt behaviour' may be observed in the live situation with a genuine patient. However, in practical terms this can, it is said, mean that as different trainees have different patients and different observers or assessors there may be wide disparity in results with possible injustice.

More recently-developed techniques of assessment may be used in which an approximation to real-life patient situations is reached with the provision of the same situation for all candidates. While these newer techniques are suitable for formal examination one cannot escape the concept that the most valid observations are those of overt behaviour made 'on the job' (Flanagan, 1954). All other methods are substitutes however closely they may approximate to reality. Fortunately in the field of vocational training the trainee is by definition in the situation for three years where his several teachers in and out of hospital may each, over several months of time, make personal observation of his overt behaviour in many situations.

This circumstance permits of the use of rating scales on a continuous or regular basis. Work currently being undertaken on the construction and use of such scales in Manchester (Byrne and Freeman, 1971) suggests that there is a good correlation between this method of assessment and the more conventionally constructed 'once and for all' assessments of universities and Royal Colleges. If, as seems likely, these early results are eventually confirmed then this method, difficult to construct but simple to apply should be a valuable aid in the problems of evaluation. Within our present overall educational system it seems difficult to support the continuation of the 'once and for all' traditional examinations for postgraduates. All our young medical graduates have nowadays successfully passed over the sequential academic hurdles of 11-plus, 'O' levels, 'A' levels, and university entrance, 2nd M.B. (that major cause of academic attrition) and the Final M.B. examinations. There is surely no need to provide further academic hurdles. Rather once a postgraduate, in our context a trainee, enters a training programme, his progress and fulfilment of the defined learning objectives are as much a measure of the effectiveness of the programme as they represent an assessment of the trainee himself.

We suggest that the progressive rating which we are to describe will serve adequately to assess the great majority of trainees. It will not, even if it be deemed necessary, separate out the individual layers of the cream. Neither will the method, while identifying frank failure, serve fairly to distinguish the narrow band of those equivocal in result. For both these relatively small groups perhaps the traditional method may be best. In addition to its value in assessment, a value which present research appears likely to confirm, progressive rating is ideally conceived for the postgraduate 'on the job' situation. It is useful, moreover, to identify early any falling off in the performance of the trainee or his learning difficulties, and is thus a valuable tool for use in his education. The following framework provides a base in which all the various skills may be displayed and it provides further a basis for assessment in terms relevant to the normal methods of performance of the clinician.

In the broadest terms the basic skills of the general practitioner lie, as do those of most clinicians, in:

1. Making a relationship with the patient
2. Gathering information
3. Identifying the patient's problems—expressed in physical, psychological and social terms
4. Proposing and/or implementing solutions to these problems.

There is yet little hard evidence of the positive identification of many of the individual skills within the broad groups referred to. An exception is the work of Anderson and Day on the skills of *history taking* (1970). They suggest that the skills of history taking are:

1. Achievement of rapport with patient
2. Achievement of maximum comprehension between patient and doctor

3. Obtaining essential information
4. Interviewing logically
5. Ability to listen
6. Ability to interrupt
7. Observation of non-verbal cues
8. Interpretation of interview.

Other research is continuing in this important area. The 'critical incident' survey conducted by Flanagan (1954) in U.S.A. defined a series of skills, but—and it was an important qualification—he said, 'We cannot place these skills in an order of priority.' We have modified the skills derived by Flanagan and are presently researching for yet nicer definition. In the meantime we rely on the following list of skills. We agree with Flanagan *et al.* on the difficulties of ascribing priorities or a ranking order to this list.

A. Skill in:
1. Managing patients
2. Teamwork
3. Delegation
4. Relating to other colleagues.

B. Skill in collecting information by:
1. History taking
2. Examination
3. The use of investigations or procedures
4. Recording information
5. The interpretation of information.

C. Skill in:
1. Decisions
2. Early diagnosis
3. Preparation of a plan for management and therapy
4. The selection of therapy
5. Emergency treatment
6. Long-term care—periodic assessment of plan.

D. Skill in interventive medicine in relation to:
1. The patient
2. The family
3. The community.

E. Skill in:
1. The organisation of his practice and himself
2. Business methods.

F. Skill in communications.

Attitudes

We should also define the basic attitudes required of the general practitioner.

The concept of 'attitude' is one of the most difficult to define, partly because it is an amorphous term having its base in many disciplines. One must distinguish between the concepts of 'attitude' and 'personality' accepting that there will be relationships between an individual's personality and the nature and content of a specific attitude. One of the most influential definitions of 'attitude'—although none is universally accepted—is that of Gordon Allport in 1935, 'Attitude is a mental and neural state of readiness organised through experience, exerting a directive or dynamic influence upon the individual's response to all objects and situations with which it is related.' Newcomb (1964), in providing a precise and authoritative statement on the definition of the concept of attitude thirty years later, found it necessary to quote Allport's definition.

While there are some leading psychologists who advance reasons for dismissing the concept of attitude there are certain practical advantages in accepting the concept as a base from which to assess certain facets of behaviour. It must though be emphasised that the study of attitudes is most adequate and effective when it is based on a study of observed overt behaviour. The argument is now familiar that there is little point in studying verbally expressed attitudes either orally or on an attitude scale since one does not know to what extent they may be reflected in relevant actions or behaviour (Byrne and Freeman, 1969).

It has been suggested that special behavioural characteristics will be related to certain types of attitudes, particularly basic ones such as *compassion* and *courtesy* (which we would regard as fundamental for the general practitioner). These relate closely to the personality trait studied among, for example, Yale medical students (Becker and Geer, 1961), such as cynicism, humanitarianism and general anxiety.

Gee and Glaser (1958) suggest that in training courses students develop a detachment and control over many of their emotional reactions and acquire a detached concern. Development of a proper degree of concern for patients will probably be a determining factor in the doctor's attitude towards, for example, aggressive patients.

Note. Those who wish to learn about the concept and measurement of attitudes should be prepared to read widely. As a *beginning* we would suggest:

1. George Miller (ed.) (1968) *Teaching and Learning in Medical School*. Harvard University Press.

2. Jahoda and Warren. *Attitudes.*
3. Lazarus and Opton. *Personality.*

Both the latter published in the Penguin Modern Psychology Series.

The following list is of those attitudes the trainee might be expected to demonstrate at the conclusion of his training. In each case the attitudes should be seen to be *favourable*, *salient* and *general.* They have been grouped under three headings:

I To patients
II To colleagues
III To aspects of professional life, including special disciplines and techniques.

I ATTITUDES TO PATIENTS WHO NEED—

1. Advice and education
2. Personal, primary and continuing care
3. Terminal care
4. Special care as vulnerable groups
5. Interventive care
6. Early diagnosis
7. Diagnosis expressed whole person, i.e. biological and social terms.

II ATTITUDES TO COLLEAGUES

1. Teamwork
2. Delegation
3. Organisation
4. Group allegiance (of patients and group members)
5. Co-workers and auxiliary staff
6. Consultants and other doctors.

III ATTITUDES TO ASPECTS OF PROFESSIONAL LIFE

1. Exhibition of sound clinical principles
2. Good recording
3. Continuing education
4. Special interest and techniques
5. Other disciplines, e.g. epidemiology, social medicine
6. The application of psychological principles to oneself and the doctor/patient relationship
7. Ethics.

The situation of the trainee again is such that the required observation of overt behaviour is regularly possible, and it enables assessment of attitudes to be made without the use of attitudinal scales or structured interviews.

We are now in a position to discuss some methods of evaluation and suggest appropriate uses of them.

Assessment of factual recall

During the training situation such assessments arise naturally, particularly if the teacher is using the Socratic style with its emphasis on teacher questioning. Inherent also in this style is the continuing opportunity to observe and monitor progress which can and should be recorded with particular reference to areas of weakness needing to be remedied.

For more formal assessment the Multiple Choice Question Paper —M.C.Q.—has a wide application. It provides a fair, reliable and well-validated method of measuring factual recall in great depth, yet on the other hand easy and objective to mark. It is also easy to machine mark and is hence suitable for large numbers of candidates. Its weaknesses are that it is of less value in the measurement of concepts and skills, is time consuming and difficult to construct and validate. Young people are accustomed—in some instances perhaps too accustomed—to the use of the M.C.G. both in school and in medical school. It is the older generation which not unnaturally is suspicious of or hostile to a method of which it knows and understands but little. Properly applied an M.C.Q. is the fairest way of measuring factual recall.

There appears to be a growing concensus that the optimum kind of M.C.Q. is the 'one out of five'. Here, from five possible answers, the examinee is asked to indicate that which, in his view, is the one appropriate answer to the question. As the examinee may also elect to make no answer at all he has six possible choices.

There are, however, two important points to be made about factual recall. One that it is sterile unless allied to the skills of proper usage, and secondly that in other methods of assessing skills there is an implied and inferred content of factual recall. A history cannot be adequately taken without some factual knowledge, for even if by chance the correct questions were asked there would still be required a base of factual recall to permit the employment of the skill of using the answers (Morris, q.v.).

It is for these reasons that contemporary theory and practice give a low weighting to factual recall in overall assessments of professional competence.

Many of the methods used in examinations such as Final M.B. and the various postgraduate diplomates serve as substitutes for 'on the job' assessment. Techniques such as the Simulated Patient Management Problem or the Simulated Consultation may present the fairest and most replicable situation for all candidates in these examinations, but we submit that in the training situations we are discussing they are irrelevant and unnecessary. Continuous assessment of the trainee at work is a superior and more relevant method.

In his learning situations the trainee may be regularly observed by each of his several teachers, who are enabled to monitor his progress and to observe at first hand the effects of teaching and training. While this book is concerned with 'person-to-person' teaching and learning in the attachment situation, it must not be forgotten that at the time of writing this period of training for general practice represents only one year out of three. The other two years are in several posts in hospital. Each teacher may use progressive rating. The general practice attachment situation, important though it is, still represents only a portion of any of the increasing numbers of three-year programmes becoming available. Trainers will find progressive rating as we describe it of particular value in the 'review' phase of the training model, q.v.

Here is, as an example, a portion of a progressive rating scale used by us in Manchester (Byrne and Freeman, 1969).

CRITERION 1 INFORMATION GATHERING

This criterion is concerned with the trainee's willingness, ability and skill in gathering information necessary for diagnosis and/or decisions.

THE UNACCEPTABLE TRAINEE
follows no routine of history taking. He fails to identify or does not bother to develop salient leads. He will not pursue alternative hypotheses. He does not seek information on clinical, psychological and social factors. His recording is sketchy and not systematic. He tends to use investigations in a 'blunderbuss' fashion.

THE ACCEPTABLE TRAINEE
takes a comprehensive history, when appropriate, including physical, psychological and social factors. He carefully makes an appropriate physical examination. He records his information carefully and uses previous and continuing records intelligently. He plans investigations and uses diagnostic services intelligently.

01	02	03	04	05	06	07	08	09	10	11	12
Poor			Marginal			Good			Excellent		

The rater is required to place a vertical line at that point of the twelve-point scale which his judgement of the trainee suggests.

This is the first of nine criteria used in the Manchester scale. Here the skills of information gathering are stated in broad outline. From these several criteria a variety of check lists may be constructed which the teacher can apply at suitable intervals. George Miller (1968) says, 'The check list and the rating scale are quite similar. The rating scale may be said to be a check list which also provides an opportunity for the observer to judge the quality as well as to note the presence of the traits included. In both . . . the performances being observed and appraised *must be divided into component dimensions* . . . .'

(The reader is recommended to this work in particular for a general review of rating scales and check lists.)

In practice there must be a compromise between the check list containing so many components as to be unmanageable or unpopular with potential raters, and being so circumscribed as to be invalid.

A check list for the trainees' capacities in history taking could be constructed then with each component being assessed on at least a five-point scale.

	1	2	3	4	5
	poor(ly)				excellent(ly)
1. To what degree does the trainee achieve rapport with his patient?					
2. Does his history adequately elaborate the patient's complaints?					
3. Does he show a capacity to listen to patients?					
4. Does he show perception in exploring alternative possibilities?					
5. Does he take a history in a logical fashion?					
6. Does he extract essential information?					
7. Does he adequately interpret the findings of his history?					
8. Does he display adequate knowledge of the clinical features of the patient's complaint?					
9. Does he show knowledge of the pathological processes involved?					

It will be observed that this check list takes note of both knowledge and skills. While many more questions may be devised the list shown covers the important skills to be assessed. Until evidence accumulates to show the validity of such methods of assessment, and it is assumed that such evidence may be found, there must be continuous experiments in the development of the method. Similar lists can be and have been constructed to check on the various skills listed previously. It is only in the situation of organised attachment that such assessments may be undertaken and hence for general practice the opportunity to do so is only beginning.

The regular use of such lists presents a continuous record of the progress of the trainee throughout his attachment. It enables weaknesses to be identified and hence permits remedial attempts. It provides the trainee with evidence of his own progress. In the summation of a series of assessments on each of the trainees involved in a programme the success or otherwise of the latter may be determined. Indeed it is possible to alter programmes while they are continuing by acting upon the evidence thus provided.

It is equally necessary to assess the trainer. In the first instance all clinical teachers should have a high degree of 'self-understanding'. While this may be in part inherent, perhaps in greater part experientially acquired, there are more objective ways for discovery. A method regularly used in many medical schools in the U.S.A. in particular is that of assessment by colleagues. They will observe lectures, seminars or tutorials for example and may then offer that constructive criticism which is necesssary and which should be accepted.

Trainees themselves must be invited—if in these days this is necessary—to provide constructive criticism. The trainer should search his mind carefully and honestly if a student(s) is performing less well than was predicted or is required. The teaching may be at fault for few 'learning blocks' in the students are culpable. Perhaps the first information of value to be acquired by the trainer, information which may only be acquired by experience of practiced situations, relates to his natural teaching style and the learning situation in which he functions best. It has been shown that many trainers who conceive that they use the Socratic style are in fact authoritarian, while it is easy to discover that some function best in the lecture, some with small groups, most in person-to-person teaching. The observations of colleagues (who may even be friends) and trainees will help to confirm or provide self-understanding. Then attempts may be made to learn other styles or to achieve competence in other situations.

It will be a responsibility of those providing and organising training programmes to acquire such information and then to deploy their trainers to the best advantage which circumstances permit. Such considerations apply less to the more intimate and usually less formal person-to-person learning situations, but even here improvements can be made only after evidence has been obtained.

Recently regular meetings of groups of trainers have been held in various parts of the country. While many of these groups have been content to learn of the educational progress and teaching methods as a proper base for development, the more experienced have been using their sessions to provide further criticism and self-understanding.

The techniques of role-playing, for example, are helpful here. In the regular courses at Manchester, where the first of a continuing series of courses in teaching methods was held in March, 1966, videotape recordings and closed-circuit television were used to provide both group- and self-learning situations. These and other techniques are all useful in helping the trainer to assess his methods.

In one sense, however, the acid test of the trainer lies in the results which he obtains. His assessment of his trainee is one measure of his results. More subjective criticism by the trainees is also useful 'feedback' for him, and such trainee opinion can be solicited by means of questionnaires, which may be administered verbally in person, for example:

Where several trainees are involved in the implementation of training programmes, they should meet together regularly for the purpose of collating and discussing information acquired by the various methods indicated and then modifying their programmes as may appear necessary. It is a custom of the day for people from other centres in the U.K. or other countries to visit and observe the programmes of colleagues. Provided the visitor has experience in a similar field, his views after or during his observation can be of considerable constructive value. On occasion such visits may be solicited, and should normally be welcome, while opportunities should always be taken by the trainer to visit other programmes himself.

Apart from the possibilities for learning, there is the necessary provision of comparison and contrast, the possibility of assessment of one's own performance and programme against the yardsticks of others

The teacher of general practice is himself a clinician and is seeking to create another clinician. Both should wish to be as good clinicians as possible. Such teachers, therefore, must not only teach well, they must practise well. They should be as equally keen to assess their practice as they should their teaching.

Keeping good clinical records is an excellent way of assessing performance and there are many sources of information about records (Eimerl and Laidlow, 1969; Weed, 1969). Whichever methods of record-keeping are used the trainer and his trainee should, from them, be able to monitor clinical performance.

In the same way the trainer should demonstrate quality in his practice premises and organisation. Both should be assessed continuously and indicated improvements made.

This kind of domestic assessment by the trainer may be looked at by external observers such as appointment committees in the light of part of their assessment of the trainer himself. One who has indifferent records, premises and organisation may justifiably be assessed at a low level as a trainer.

Many trainers will wish to undertake research. This may be in operational, clinical, epidemiological, social or other areas, but the fact that active research is being pursued is of itself important. Teaching and research are largely interdependent. The teacher cannot subscribe to Jean Piaget's, 'The principal goal of education is to create men who are capable of doing new things . . .' unless he himself is aware of the need for doing new things. Actively pursued research is a valid way of demonstrating such an awareness, particularly if some of the research is into those educational processes in which he takes part.

The ultimate practical purpose of assessment of the trainer is to provide the evidence upon which change may be effected. There is no point in undertaking assessment for its own sake. Hence the trainer must be assiduous in his own continuing education, using any or all methods from the wide range of contemporary possibilities. Quite apart from the fact that he will maintain and improve his own competence in an era of rapid and important developments he may at the same time condition his trainee to acquire a similar attitude to learning. This is without doubt an attitude to be taught by example—much more than by precept.

Finally, there are two points crucial to the topic of assessment and evaluation which must be made. The first is that at the moment attachment in vocational training is to a large degree experimental and must be evaluated. The second is that in the large-scale training exercises envisaged there is an implicit need for a professional educational, as well as a medical approach.

The dedicated enthusiasm of the amateur trainer, for that is what most of us general practitioners are, should be strengthened by the professional approach which recognises, accepts and fulfils the duty of assessment of our programmes, of our trainees, and of ourselves.

REFERENCES

ANDERSON, J., DAY, J. *et al.* (1970) The definition and evaluation of the skills required to obtain a patient's history of illness: the use of videotape recordings. *Postgraduate Medical Journal*, **46,** 606–12.

BASS, B. M. (1965) *Organisational Psychology*. Boston: Allyn & Bacon.

BECKER, H. S. & GEER, B. (1961). The fate of idealism in medical school. In *Sociology: The Progress of a Decade*, edited by S. Lipset and N. Smelser, pp. 293–7. New York: Prentice Hall.

BLOOM, B. S. (1956) *Taxonomy of Educational Objectives*. London: Longman.

BROWNE, K. & FREELING, P. (1967) *Doctor–Patient Relationship*. Edinburgh: Livingstone.

BYRNE, P. S. & FREEMAN, J. (1969) *Bases for Evaluation of Training Programmes in General Practice*. Departmental Memo. Department of General Practice, University of Manchester.

BYRNE, P. S. & FREEMAN, J. (1971*a*) Clinical Factual Recall in General Practice. *British Journal of Medical Education*, **5,** No. 2, 118–124.

BYRNE, P. S. & FREEMAN, J. (1971*b*) Postgraduate training for general practice: an assessment of aptitudes and abilities of trainee entrants. *British Journal of Medical Education*, **5** (4), 293–304.

CROMBIE, D. W. (1963) *Medical Care*, **1,** 92.

DEWALD, P. A. (1964) *Psychotherapy—a Dynamic Approach*. Oxford: Blackwells.

DEWEY, J. (1959) *Dewey on Education*. Teachers' College, Columbia.

DEWEY, J. (1961) *Democracy and Education*. New York: The Macmillan Company.

EIMERL, T. S. & LAIDLOW, A. J. (eds) (1969) *Research in General Practice*. Edinburgh: Livingstone.

EUROPEAN RESEARCH GROUP ON MANAGEMENT (1967) *A Program of Exercizes in Organisational Psychology*, 3rd edition. Brussels.

EVANS, E. G. S. (1969) *Modern Educational Psychology*. London: Routledge & Kegan Paul.

FLANAGAN, J. D. (1954) The critical incident technique. *Psychological Bulletin*, **51,** 326–58.

FRANKENA, W. E. (1965) *Three Historical Philosophies of Education*. Glenview, Illinois: Scott Foresman.

FULTON, A. E. (1970) The measurement of speaker credibility. *The Journal of Communication*, **20,** 270–9.

GAGE, N. L. (1963) *Handbook of Research on Teaching*. Chicago: Rand McNally.

GEE, H. H. & GLASER, R. J. (eds) (1958) The ecology of the medical student. *Journal of Medical Education*, **33,** 10 (part 2).

JAHODA, M. & WARREN, N. (1966) *Attitudes*. Penguin Modern Psychology Series. Harmondsworth, Middx: Penguin.

KAHN, R. L. & CANNELL, C. F. (1957) *The Dynamics of Interviewing*. New York: Wiley.

KERSH, B. Y. (1958) The adequacy of meaning as an explanation for the superiority of learning by independent discovery. *Journal of Educational Psychology*, **49,** 282–92.

KUETHE, J. L. (1968) *The Teaching–Learning Process*. Glenview, Illinois: Scott Foresman.

LAZARUS, R. S. & OPTON, E. M. (1967) *Personality*. Penguin Modern Psychology Series. Harmondsworth, Middx: Penguin.

LONG, B. E. L. (1969) A theoretical model for method selection. *Industrial Training International*, **4** (11), 475–8.

McLEISH, J. (1968) *The Lecture Method*. Monograph. Cambridge: Institute of Education.

MILLER, G. E. (ed.) (1968) *Teaching and Learning in Medical School*. Cambridge, Mass.: Harvard University Press.

MILLER, N. E. & DOLLARD, J. (1941) *Social Learning and Imitation*. New Haven: Yale University Press.

MORENO, J. L. (1934) *Who Shall Survive?* Washington, D.C.: Nervous and Mental Disease Publ. Co.

MORRIS, J. F. & LUNZER, E. A. (1968) *Development in Human Learning*. London: Staples Press.

MOULY, G. J. (1968) *Psychology for Effective Teaching*, pp. 553–4. New York: Holt, Reinhart & Winston.

O.E.C.D. (1969) *The Discovery Method: An International Experiment in Retraining*. Paris: Belbin.

ROGERS, C. (1965) *Client Centred Therapy*. Boston: Houghton Mifflin.

ROGERS, C. (ed.) (1969) *Teaching on Equal Terms*, pp. 11–21. B.B.C.

ROYAL COLLEGE OF GENERAL PRACTITIONERS (1969) Future needs of the General Practitioner. *Journal of the Royal College of General Practitioners*, **18,** 358.

SHERTZER, B. & STONE, S. C. (1968) *Fundamentals of Counselling*. Boston: Houghton Mifflin.

SHULMAN, L. S. & KEISLAR, E. R. (1966) *Learning by Discovery. A Critical Appraisal*. Chicago: Rand McNally.

SKINNER, B. F. (1958) *Science and Human Behaviour*. New York: The Macmillan Company.

THOMPSON, G. C. & HUNNICUTT, C. W. (1944) The effect of praise or blame on the work achievement of 'introverts' and 'extroverts'. *Journal of Educational Psychology*, **35,** 257–66.

WEED, L. L. (1969) *Medical Education, Medical Records and Patient Care*. Division of Research in Medical Education, Western School of Medicine, Western Reserve University, Cleveland, Ohio.

INDEX